The Pen of a Ready Writer

by

Becky DeWitt

BDIG Publishing

Printed in the United States of America

First Printing: June 2022

ISBN-9798838729293

PREFACE

The Pen is a compilation of prophetic writings over a six-year period. Listening for words from the throne room and dedication were required for such a great assignment. These words contain revelation that speaks to the heart of a Believer regardless of the time or date that they were given and written. There is an impact and mark that cannot be erased. They are filled with spirit and life.

COMING FOR YOUR WORDS

What are you speaking today that an angel from heaven will be dispatched to hear the voice of God coming through an earthly vessel that is filled with the spirit of the Almighty? These are the days to let your words be few and let His Word come through.

For He is watching over His Word to perform it in your life. There shall be a performance because you have believed and kept the faith not wavering and solid confidence in the Lord your God. For you have believed that He is able to do this. For you did not look at the natural, at that which was, but to Him and what was to be.

Call those things that be not in the earth from the heavens. Much is waiting on you for the release. Only you can do this by your faith. For it has already been released from His hand. Call those things that you have never imagined. Prepare to receive my thoughts and act upon that which I give. It shall come to pass and manifest, amazing and astounding you. For you shall say, "I never imagined, but God." My glory shall be revealed in the days ahead like never before.

The angels, they stand ready, waiting and watching. They are coming for my words.

"Then he said to me, Fear not, Daniel, for from the first day that you set your mind and heart to understand and to humble yourself before your God, your words were heard, and I have come as a consequence of [and in response to] your words." (Daniel 10:12 AMP).

"And blessed, happy,[l]to be envied is she who believed that there would be a fulfillment of the things that were spoken to her from the Lord." (Luke 1:45 AMP).

"When He reached the house and went in, the blind men came to Him, and Jesus said to them, Do you believe that I am able to do this? They said to Him, Yes, Lord." (Matthew 9:28 AMP).

"Do not, therefore, fling away your fearless confidence, for it carries a great and glorious compensation of reward." (Hebrews 10:35 AMP).

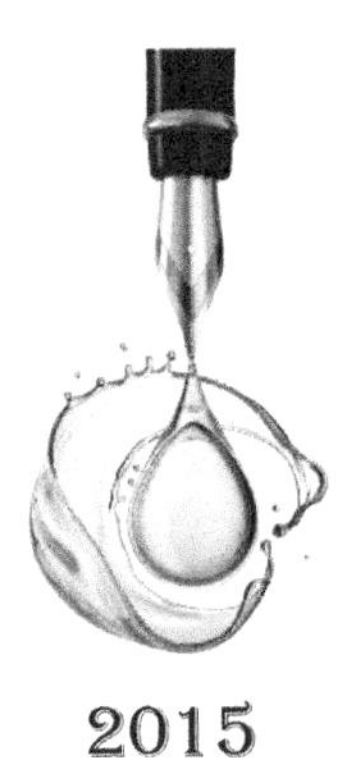

2015

CALL

CALL – to request, to summon, to ask, to invite.

I have called you to be by my side, to walk with me, to talk with me. Where are you? You are not in position. I have much to pour into you, but you must be in position. Do not allow the enemy to take you any further. Stop him NOW! You have allowed him to displace and distract you. Now is the time for you to refocus. Get up and get back where I have placed you. Do not allow anyone or anything to move you. Set your eyes like dove's eyes on me alone, and then you will see. You want to see something different, keep your eyes on me.

Keep your eyes lifted and you will see time open into eternity. You may say 'what has happened to me?' Another stage of preparation. Come out of the old and into the new. It is new to you, but prepared before the foundation of everything that you see. Look up and see beyond where you are. My love will cause you to see the greater. Do not measure or compare what I do with you to anyone else. The cause is for the greater effect, the fruit that will remain for many that will come to taste, see, and know of my goodness.

"He who dwells in the shelter of the Most High Will remain secure and rest in the shadow of the Almighty whose power no enemy can withstand."
Psalm 91:1 AMP.

"Blessed is the one whom You choose and bring near To dwell in Your courts. We will be filled with the goodness of Your house, Your holy temple. By awesome and wondrous things You answer us in righteousness, O God of our salvation, You who are the trust and hope of all the ends of the earth and of the farthest sea;"
Psalm 65:4-5 AMP.

"For nothing is hidden, except to be revealed; nor has anything been kept secret, but that it would come to light that is, things are hidden only temporarily, until the appropriate time comes for them to be known." Mark 4:22 AMP.

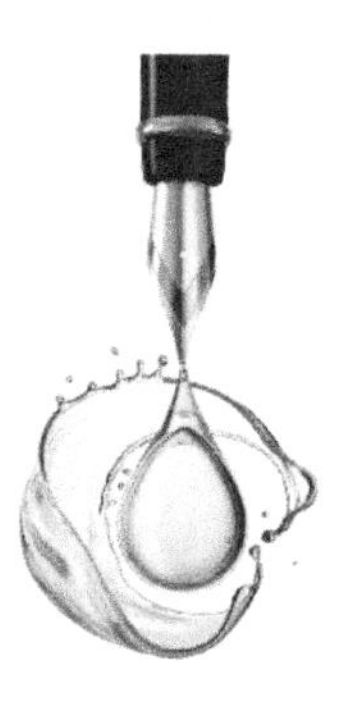

2016

INHERITANCE

Do not worry about your earthly inheritance. For what I give is far beyond that you can imagine. Is not the inheritance through the BLOOD of my SON greater than that of man? I, who have formed you, know you, your thoughts, your needs, and your desires. I will fulfill my plan for your life. Look not to man but unto me. I see your tears. Do not ever think that I do not see you and everything around you.

Look up and see the glory of your heavenly Father, who daily provides for you. There is nothing that can compare to my inheritance. My inheritance is a KINGDOM inheritance. Weep no more, cry no more, because you are in lack. Look past your past and see the abundance of your future. For I know your name and I have not forgotten about you. You are on my timetable.

Think on my goodness, my grace as my BLESSING is due to arrive sooner than you think. Think SUPERNATURALLY NOW! For your inheritance is far greater that you can ever imagine.

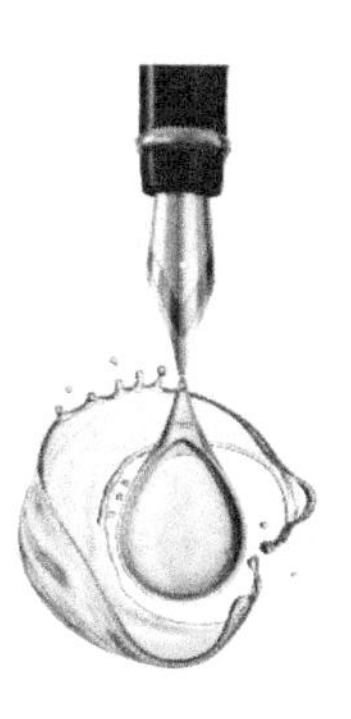

2016

BUILD

Build yourself up on your most holy faith it is not your faith, but my faith which was once delivered to you in a measure. For it is this faith that will keep you in days to come. I AM speaking mysteries of the Kingdom to all who would hear. These mysteries propel you into your destiny that I have prepared. It was made ready and kept ready long ago before the foundation of the world. SEE NOW. Lift your eyes and SEE NOW. All of heaven is watching.

The weapons that I have given you are not carnal, but mighty THROUGH ME to pull down every stronghold. For I AM your exceeding great reward. Sound the alarm. Make ready. For you are an overcomer. That which you experienced in time will be overshadowed by great exceeding joy.

For I AM your joy and your strength. I know your name and you have not denied me despite the attacks over time. I AM your exceeding great reward. Never forget the price that was paid for you, My BELOVED. You shall see my goodness and my glory in the land of the living. Watch and SEE. Expect me. Lift your eyes and SEE my arrival is imminent.

"But you, beloved, build yourselves up founded on your most holy faith, make progress, rise like an edifice higher and higher, praying in the Holy Spirit;"
Jude 20 AMPC

"I will move past my enemies with this one, sure hope: ***that with my own eyes, I will see the goodness of the Eternal in the land of the living."***
Psalm 27:13 The Voice

"The weapons of the war we're fighting are not of this world but are powered by God and effective at tearing down the strongholds erected against His truth. We are

demolishing arguments and ideas, every high-and-mighty philosophy that pits itself against the knowledge of the one true God. We are taking prisoners of every thought, every emotion, and subduing them into obedience to theAnointed One."
2 Corinthians 10:4-5 The Voice

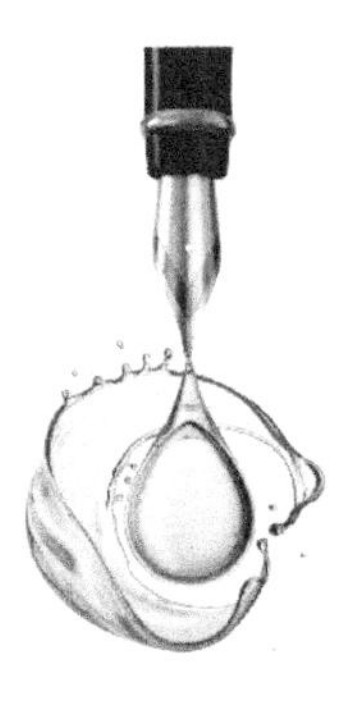

2016

FULFILLMENT

I shall FULFILL MY WORD in your life. It is the time for every vision. They will no longer be prolonged. For I have spoken it, shall I not make it good? Many wait and say 'when is He coming?' I AM already there. I AM in the next thought and idea. I AM in everything concerning you.

Know this, I AM that I AM is with you. Will I leave you? NEVER! Can I leave you? NEVER! You are mine, my prized possession and I make up the jewels for display. It is time for you to come into the fullness of your purpose. I have designed it. I AM the one who ordains destiny. You have asked for much and that you will receive and be the display of my glory upon my favored ones. One thing I desire that you stay in my house all the days that are before you. Never leave or forsake the gifts that I have given you. My pen is writing the NEW upon your heart and you shall see those things that I have written. I AM not finished. I AM just beginning. You will see and they will see MY GLORY.

"Son of man, what is this proverb that you have in the land of Israel, saying, The days drag on and every vision comes to nothing and is not fulfilled? Tell them therefore, Thus says the Lord God: I will put an end to this proverb, and they shall use it no more as a proverb in Israel. But say to them, The days are at hand and the fulfillment of every vision."
Ezekiel 12:22-23 AMPC

"For the vision is yet for an appointed time and it hastens to the end fulfillment; it will not deceive or disappoint. Though it tarry wait earnestly for it, because it will surely come; it will not be behind hand on its appointed day."
Habakkuk 2:3 AMPC

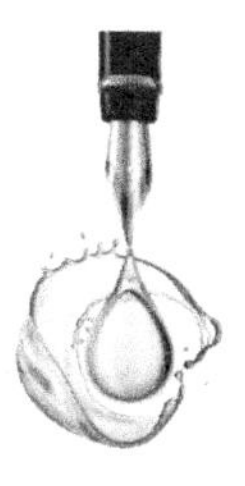

2016

ENDURANCE

ENDURANCE - The ability, strength and power to continue or last, especially despite fatigue, stress, or other adverse conditions, hardships or trials.

If the enemy could have done what he wanted to do, it would have been done by now. But the Father equipped us in eternity before He released us into time. That is why greater is He that is in you than he that is in the world and we wear the whole amour of GOD. Even though your endurance has the attention of heaven and hell, you have the VICTORY.

For there are more with you than there are against you. My angels have charge over you. I have given you power to tread upon serpents, scorpions and all power of the enemy. Even when the enemy thinks that he is attacking you, he is really attacking me. When you wear my armor, you are wearing me and it is tailor made for every Believer. You will STAND and not be shaken.

"Take with me your share of the hardships and suffering which you are called to endure as a good first-class soldier of Christ Jesus. No soldier when in service gets entangled in the enterprises of civilian life; his aim is to satisfy and please the one who enlisted him."
2 Timothy 2:3-4

"Therefore put on God's complete armor, that you may be able to resist and stand your ground on the evil day of danger, and, having done all the crisis demands, to stand firmly in your place."
Ephesians 6:13

THE PEN

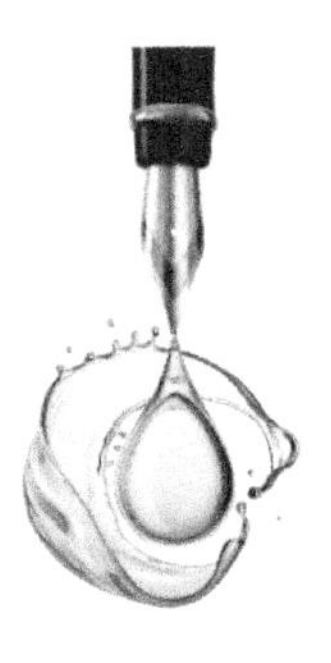

2016

PECULIAR TREASURE

Peculiar Treasures are rare finds that are hidden for an appointed time. They have been chosen and marked for His use. He has created them to hunger for Him. Rare as diamonds surviving pressure and time to be created a new. That shall shine brightly in the days to come and in right alignment with His will when He releases them suddenly. They will not be dull in any way but display His brilliance in every way for He will illumine them. A light blinding for all to see. And it will be known that it is the Lord with them shining and displaying His glory.

For He is purifying His vessels for the greater anointing. The darkness of the enemy has increased in the earth, but it will not prevail. This purification is a process that must take place NOW to enter into the NEW. You are being prepared for a NEW walk. Your walk will be different from before and deeper than before. How far you want to go and the depth is up to you as you seek after me with all your heart. Prepare for the LEAP as you are being LAUNCHED.

" Now therefore, if you will obey My voice in truth and keep My covenant, then you shall be My own peculiar possession and treasure from among and above all peoples; for all the earth is Mine. And you shall be to Me a kingdom of priests, a holy nation consecrated, set apart to the worship of God."

Exodus 19:5-6 AMP

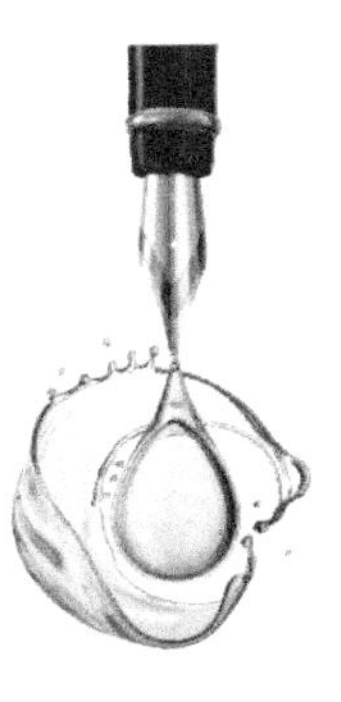

2016

THE OPEN DOOR

I am on the other side waiting for you to enter in. Let my wind move you, bring you and present you. Arrival is eminent. Open your eyes and see all that I have prepared for you for this season. Oh, the wonder, the joy that is upon your face. You never imagined.

You say, 'No Lord, I didn't. I was just trying to keep the faith.' But you did and all is not lost. But there was much to gain. The lips of the righteous shall feed many. I am drawing you closer. I am call you to come up higher to see. For the glory of the Lord shall cover the earth as the waters cover the sea.

"Take a look at the nations and watch what happens! You will be shocked and amazed. For in your days, I am doing a work, a work you will never believe even if someone tells you plainly!"
Habakkuk 1:5 The Voice

"I see what you've done. Now see what I've done. I've opened a door before you that no one can slam shut. You don't have much strength, I know that; you used what you had to keep my Word. You didn't deny me when times were rough."
Revelation 3:8 MSG

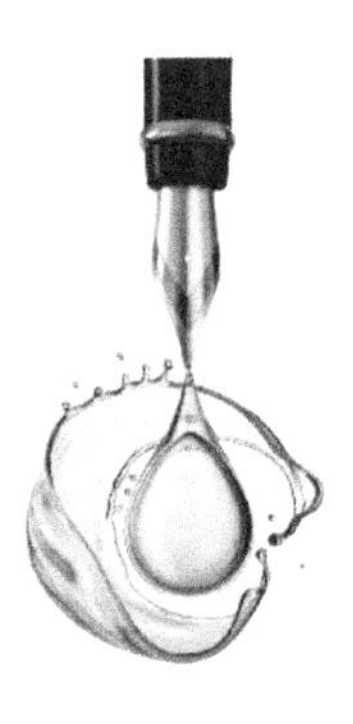

2016

SPONTANEOUS SOUND

"Spontaneous Sound" is one that flows from the heart and rehearsed. You cannot rehearse this. It is fresh and it flows like a river. It rages against the enemy of your soul. Start out simple and watch for me to come in. I love the sound of your heart, not your lips. Every time you worship, a cleansing in your heart takes place. What you are saying to the world and what you are saying to me is that the I AM that I AM is the only one for me. And sometimes you will not be able to turn it off. Don't even try. You will be ***"captured"*** in My Presence.

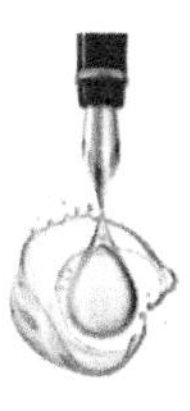

2016

SHOWTIME

The curtain is being pulled back and opened for view of what GOD has done! That stillness has RESET you more than you can ever imagine! You thought you were just being still and you were being MEASURED for the NEW garment! DRESSED FOR YOUR DESTINY!!! Only a few will be able to VIEW the NEW you! It is time for the NEXT! NEXT - immediately following in time, place or position.

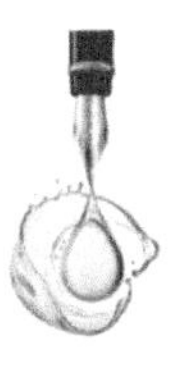

2016

SEE TO SEE

Kingdom Citizens of the Most High GOD. There is a shaking going on in you, around you and through you. I am shaking and pushing pack the darkness. For no evil will come nigh your dwelling place. Kingdom Citizen of the Most High GOD, I am shaking you. It is I who is shaking you. I am shaking everything out of you that would keep you from coming into the prepared place in my presence. I am waiting for you.

Now is the time to come up. Come up higher. Come up higher. All of heaven awaits your arrival for you to see the treasures that are reserved in your name. Yes, they have been reserved from the beginning of time. I reserved them and put your name on them before your birth, before I released you from eternity into time. I am the One who releases.

"After this I looked, and behold, a door standing open in heaven! And the first voice which I had heard addressing me like the calling of a war trumpet said, Come up here, and I will show you what must take place in the future. At once I came under the Holy Spirit's power, and behold, a throne stood in heaven, with One seated on the throne! And He Who sat there appeared like the crystalline brightness of jasper and the fiery sardius, and encircling the throne there was a halo that looked like a rainbow of emerald."
Revelation 4:1-3 AMPC

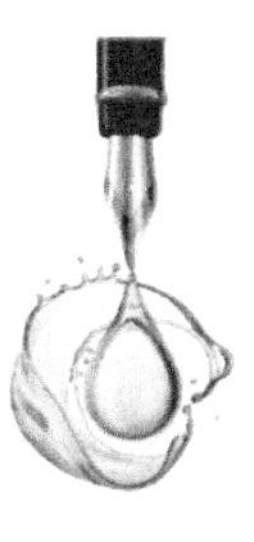

2017

THOUGHTS

"I want to deal with the mind of my people. These are the days of much revelation. If only they would seek me. For I am the giver of truth and of life. For I can put my mind in your mind. Yes, my thoughts are not your thoughts because you have been limited in your thinking. The enemy has done this. It is all a part of his plan. He is after your mind because it is the center of creativity. Do you not know that when you receive my thoughts that the creative process begins. I Am the Creator of all things. It is through your connection with me in the Spirit that I can download the things of heaven that I have plan to exist on the earth.

I need you to come up into your rightful place. Your rightful place of Kings and Priests in the earth. Use your authority for I have given it to you. Use it NOW! For the Kingdom is advancing. There will be signs, wonders, and miracles in the days to come that many will be in awe. I will showcase and demonstrate what I can do through you and with you. Many are about finances. For am I not the God of it all. The heavens and the earth are mine. I will do what I said I will do. In my time, not yours. Time only exists as I allow it. For I Am the one who created it. I Am the Creator of all things. I Am Eternal. I Am God and there is no other.

So, watch now and see as even the heavens display my glory. Creativity is mine and I will give it to whom I please in the days to come for the great wealth transfer. There will be a great wealth transfer. I Am calling my children to their rightful place. It shall be seen and it shall be known and many will wonder how, why, and when. I will put their minds in awe. By awesome and terrible things shall my answers come that terrify the wicked. If I spoke it, shall I not also do it? I Am the Lord and all creation knows my voice.

Hear now and obey and prepare. Get up. Get ready for the rain of abundance in areas that you have not even thought of. Prepare for new thoughts. Prepare for new wisdom. Prepare for new knowledge. Prepare for new understanding. Prepare yourself for inventions and ideas are coming. There is not impossibility, doubt or unbelief in my thoughts. My thoughts contain possibility coded within with the mysteries and secrets of the universe from its Creator. It is time to advance my Kingdom in the earth."

"I don't think the way you think. The way you work isn't the way I work." God's Decree. "For as the sky soars high above earth, so the way I work surpasses the way you work, and the way I think is beyond the way you think."
Isaiah 55:8-9 MSG

O Lord, how great are thy works! and thy thoughts are very deep.
Psalm 92:5 KJV

"I always pray that the God of our Lord Jesus Christ, the Father of glory, may grant you a spirit of wisdom and of revelation that gives you a deep and personal

and intimate insight into the true knowledge of Him, for we know the Father through the Son. And I pray that the eyes of your heart, the very center and core of your being may be enlightened, flooded with light by the Holy Spirit, so that you will know and cherish the hope, the divine guarantee, the confident expectation to which He has called you, the riches of His glorious inheritance in the saints, God's people."
Ephesians 1:17-18 AMP

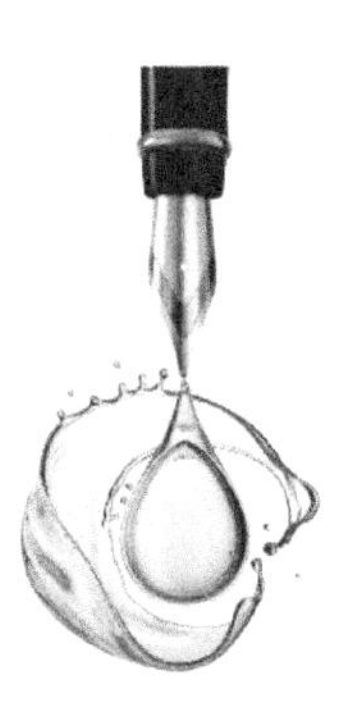

2017

PURPOSE

For it is MY PURPOSE that you live now and see MY PURPOSE is your life's existence. Yes, I AM dealing with you about your PURPOSE. Is must be clear to you now. It must be understood. It is beyond that what you can imagine. Do you think that I, the GOD of the universe created you without a PURPOSE? Everything that I created has PURPOSE. PURPOSE is embedded within. It may not be seen initially, but you have to look deep within. It is not visible to the naked eye, but only to the spiritual eye. I AM lifting the veil off of your eyes and others as well. See and you shall see. See and you shall see beyond the natural. Say what you see. See the path of MY PURPOSE. It all ends well. There is not a day that does not include MY PURPOSE.

My Kingdom mysteries have PURPOSE that I want to reveal. They cannot be revealed to those who do not understand MY PURPOSE. It is MY PURPOSE that will prevail, not man's. For everything, that I have done has PURPOSE. And the things that will be done are already done with MY PURPOSE. What you see is the eternal released into time. You think that I AM doing it, but it has already been done, MY PURPOSE.

Are you willing to give up your way, your purpose for MY WAY, MY PURPOSE? MY PURPOSE stands against everything. MY PURPOSE unfolds DESTINY. MY PURPOSE overrides time because it is eternal. How many will understand their true PURPOSE?

Everything that lives and dies has PURPOSE. Look now through the lens of PURPOSE. For I will equip your eyes now to see with PURPOSE, not just for the now, but for that which is to come. See the connection. Connect the dots for the picture. There is a domino effect. I AM the life giver and when I give life, you can also give life. Spread your wings. Spread MYWORD. Spread life in ME. Empty out and I will fill you again and again.

Are you ready for the new? The new is MY PURPOSE. Understand it, see it, and walk it out. Walk in MY PURPOSE, not yours so that you will see many manifestations and evidence of MY PURPOSE for your life. I AM waiting for your "YES". MY Son had HIS PURPOSE and it was for you. Understand my love and you will understand MY PURPOSE. MY love is in it all. It is written. Pursue MY PURPOSE for MY Promises are written.

"In Him we also were made God's heritage (portion) and we obtained an inheritance; for we had been foreordained (chosen and appointed beforehand) in accordance with His purpose, Who works out everything in agreement with the counsel and design of His own will."
Ephesians 1:11 AMPC

"I know what I'm doing. I have it all planned out—plans to take care of you, not abandon you, plans to give you the future you hope for."
Jeremiah 29:11 MSG

"Then I said, Behold, here I am, coming to do Your will, O God, to fulfill what is written of Me in the volume of the Book."
Hebrews 10:12 AMPC

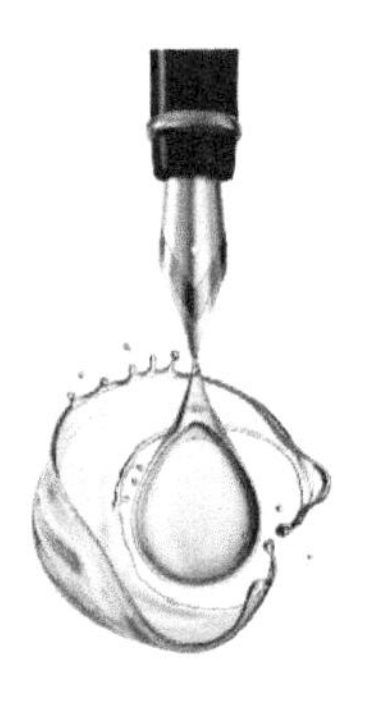

2017

THE HOLY KISS

AWAKEN, AWAKEN, MY BELOVED. For I have AWAKENED and SEALED YOU. YOU ARE MINE Listen to the beat of my heart. Rest in me. For it is in me and through me that you obtain rest. RESET NOW for I am with you. I watch over you. I have watched over you from eternity into time.

YOU ARE MINE. Yes, you are and you always were. I am calling you. Take my hand and come with me. Come up into my high places and see the wonder, the beauty of it all designed for you. The longing that you feel, it is for me. Nothing will ever satisfy or take my place. Be still and know that I am your God. You are not wandering and you are not lost.

I AM the Great Shepherd who watches over you and Jehovah Immeku, for I am with you. Jehovah Qanna, I am jealous over you and for you. Come to me now and rest with a Holy Kiss. I bless you and seal you unto myself. YOU ARE MINE. Before there was a foundation of the world, you were mine and will always be mine.

As your eyes move across these words, see my love for you, hear my love for you, feel my love for you as it overflows from my throne. A heavenly touch for your heart that can never be compared. Come unto me MY BELOVED. I am calling you closer than ever before. Feel my heartbeat for you. You are my prized possession. Hear me calling you. I am just a breath away. My heart aches for you and your touch. Touch my WORD and feel me. For I am touched by your words.

Quiet yourself now while I cover you with something new. Newness in your life, which will never be the same. For I have ordained the time and it is NOW. Watch and See. Expect me with a Holy Expectation. For I will no longer withhold myself from you. More is coming. The more of me that you hunger for is coming. It is written from my heart and upon your heart to see and know the place that I am calling you to.

"Because the One who made you will be your husband; the One called Commander of heavenly armies Will set you right again, the Holy One of Israel. It's not for nothing that He is called "God of all the earth."
Isaiah 54:5 The Voice

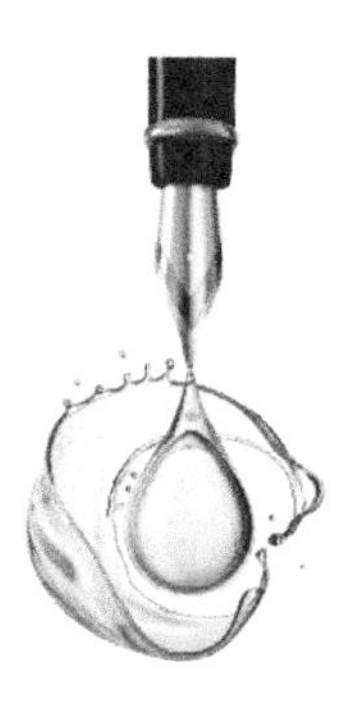

2017

WHISPER

Your hand will become my hand. Your eyes will become my eyes. Your mouth will become my mouth. My people shall do great exploits. This is the beginning of the time of great exploits. Many will see the signs, wonders, and miracles that I have longed for my people. Many will believe the signs, wonders and miracles. This is the beginning of that time that I have ordained. They will see and they will see. What I have ordained cannot be hindered or stopped.

Come closer and see. I will give you a glimpse of my plan. Only I can let you see the future. Only I can give you my sight. Come loser. Come closer. I am calling you to come closer. Many are listening but they are not hearing my call. It comes in a gentle **whisper**. Do not miss the call. I Am **whispering** in the ears of my Beloved to come closer beside me. The bedchambers are prepared for my bride. Make ready. Make haste. Make ready. Make haste. For I Am coming in a new way.

Prepare for my visitation. Even in the night season. **"UNPRECEDENTED".** Like never before. Who hath heard such a thing? Who hath seen such a thing? Like never before. It shall be daunting. I Am even going to change your vocabulary so that the words that you will speak will become more effective in the atmospheres. Change. Change. It is all about the change that is coming forth. Many will not see or understand because they are not in a place. Because they did not heed the call to come closer when I called. I Am still calling. I Am still calling. I will give them time. Not much more. I continue to **whisper** in their ears. Come. Closer. Come closer.

You have seen my hands. I Am reaching for you to come closer. It is all about coming closer beside me. What do you expect to see? See me. I Am all that you need to see. Just see me. Come closer now. For I Am still waiting for you. Closer, Closer, Closer, I Am **whispering** in your ear. Listen, Listen, Listen.

I Am moving in the gentle sweet **whisper**. Flowing from my fountain of love for you. It is in the overflow. The river is raging. Nothing will hold back what I have for you. It is time. Now is the time. Listen to the whispers of my love for you. Hear and be obedient as I direct you. Listen for the Divine Direction as I go before you to bring you into the place that I have prepared for you. It is ready Will you not come closer? Are you ready: Listen, Listen, Listen. I Am speaking gently in the **whisper**.

Come up and see all that I have prepared for you. Arrival is imminent. I am waiting to display my glory. I Am gathering the ones appointed for this time. I am gathering. Hear me when I call. It is in the **whisper**. I am in the **whisper**.

"The sheep that are My own hear and are listening to My voice; and I know them, and they follow Me." (John 10:27 AMPC).

"And He said, Go out and stand on the mount before the Lord. And behold, the Lord passed by, and a great and strong wind rent the mountains and broke in pieces the rocks before the Lord, but the Lord was not in the wind; and after the wind an earthquake, but the Lord was not in the earthquake; And after the earthquake a fire, but the Lord was not in the fire; and after the fire, a sound of gentle stillness and a still, small voice. When Elijah heard the voice, he wrapped his face in his mantle and went out and stood in the entrance of the cave. And behold, there came a voice to him and said, What are you doing here, Elijah?"

(Kings 19:11-13 AMPC).

Part 2

Oil is flowing. Mantles are falling. I Am cloaking many in this season with what has been kept back for such a time as this. They are battle ready. Elite warriors are coming forth from the unknown places walking in the **"UNPRECEDENTED".** I Am calling and they are coming closer. It is a clarion call on a frequency that is unknown. It is the **UNCOMPROMISED**.

They know who they are and are answering the call. It is our secret and they have been well hidden. But as I call them, they shall come forth. Blazing with fire, burning brightly. I have activated them through my **whisper.**

I Am even **whispering** as you read these words. Hear me now. Come up. Come closer. Come up. Come closer. In my presence so you can hear my **whisper.** New instructions and new wisdom to be released. I say unto you now, he that hath ears let him hear.

2017

COVENANT KEEPING GOD

I Am a covenant keeping GOD. I do not alter the things that have gone forth from my lips. I keep my promises for they are Yea and Amen. From everlasting to everlasting, I am GOD and GOD alone. Forever it is settled in heaven and sealed by the blood of Jesus.

I know those that are mine and make up my jewels for display. It is time for those who have been hidden,

hidden and polished to come forth and shine brightly with brilliance of the Son.

For I Am not a GOD who is afar. I am right there with you. See and know my presence in the past, present and future. I see and I know all things. For I Am GOD and GOD alone. You have heard my voice, NOW give heed to MY WORDS.

The heavens declare my glory and they shall declare MY WORD in your life. For it shall come to pass. For I Am a covenant keeping GOD. See, know and expect me in all things that transpire.

My hand is upon you and every situation. Recognize my presence in even the smallest detail. For I Am there in the midst of everything. Stay in my hand. Do not let go my hand. For I Am leading you to the greater. The greater is coming upon you. For I have scheduled it for this time in your life.

My glory will be revealed. My glory will be revealed. It is all for my glory. Do not let doubt and fear have access to your mind. For where I Am taking you is greater than you can imagine.

Lift your eyes now and see. It is because of my love for you that I can no longer wait to display my love. Your times are in my hand.

For I Am the LORD thy GOD and I do whatever I please in the heavens, the earth and the seas. From generation to generation, I am a Covenant keeping GOD.

"My covenant will I not break or profane, nor alter the thing that is gone out of My lips." Psalm 89:34

"For ever, O Lord, thy word is settled in heaven." Psalm 119:89

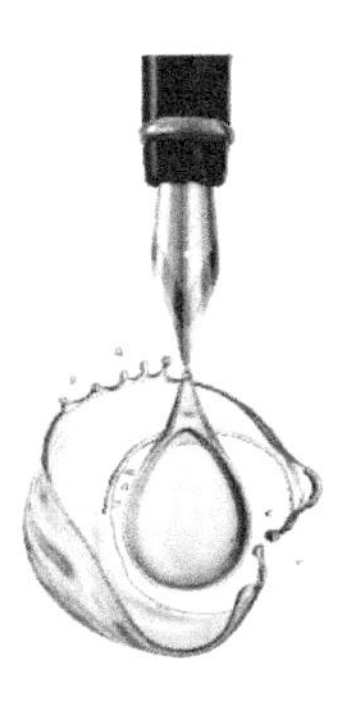

2017

OPTICAL FUSION

Kingdom Assets, Triumphant Reserve, awaken and arise to the move of God. I Am calling you close so that you can see as I see. You are seated in heavenly places so that you can see. It is your rightful place. Prepare to see as I see. I will give you a glimpse. Give me your eyes. Give me your heart and I will give you my eyes.

Open the eyes of your heart and see me for who I really am to you. This is the time that I have set for you to experience me like never before. It is the time. It is my time not yours or anyone else's or the world's. It is mine. For it is all mine Awaken, Awaken and Arise my Triumphant Ones who are my reserve. For I have placed within you the seed of righteousness that cannot be contained or contaminated.

Awaken, Awaken and Arise Now. Revolution. For I have need of you Now! Revolution. Reprimand. You are released. My sons and daughters should know me in a different all-consuming way that has not been known to them ever. I bring new light and new revelation. I bring the new to all who would receive.

"Then Elisha prayed, Lord, I pray You, open his eyes that he may see. And the Lord opened the young man's eyes, and he saw, and behold, the mountain was full of horses and chariots of fire round about Elisha."
2 Kings 6:17 AMP

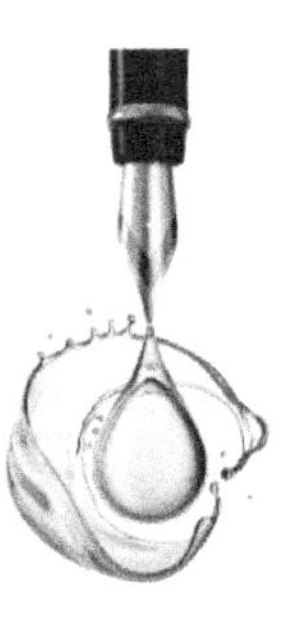

2017

THE WAVE

The WAVE is coming. Prepare yourself. My glory shall cover the earth as the waters cover the sea. You have only felt the drops of the rain of my presence. Prepare for the flood of my glory. I shall flood in unusual places that are dry and thirsty for my presence. It is about the thirsty ones.

Do not look for me in crowded places. For I Am filling a people that no one knows about, the little known who are so hungry and so thirsty. Those who hunger and thirst after might righteousness there is a filling. A filling of my glory. Watch now. It is my glory that shall cover.

The WAVE is coming. Prepare yourself. The WAVE is coming. All shall see and know that it is the presence of the Lord thy God. What do you think happens in my glory? Change, Sudden, Change.

Prepare to be caught up. Release yourself to me. Free yourself from the confinements of the enemy. Come up. Come up higher. See beyond what you see. You say, I want to see something different. Come up and you shall see. Come up so the scales can be removed. The scales cannot exist in my glory. The WAVE is coming and it will sweep you from – into. You may ask from what to what? Let your faith fill the empty space. Let your faith be unlimited.

Do not limit me, the Unlimited One. I AM taking you from your past and present into your future suddenly. The wave comes and breaks and destroys everything of the enemy's devices against you. Nothing can withstand the fury of the WAVE. The WAVE is huge because it has been building for a long time. The WAVE is coming. It is upon us. Prepare yourself. Make ready my Bride.

Part 2

The WAVE of my people is coming. Are you ready to receive them? Can you receive them in love, in my love? Will you love them as I love you? I loved you before you came to me and I love them. They are coming because they are marked for this time. They are in my WAVE and I am ushering them in. I have not rejected them and do not reject them. All are mine. I see and know all. Now is their appointed time. Make ready.

Be ready for they are coming in the WAVE of my glory. Many will not believe and have a revival fire burning brightly for all to see. The spark is ignited in the WAVE. Make yourself ready my Bride for they are coming. See the multitudes upon multitudes of every nation coming into the Kingdom. The WAVE is upon you. Sign, Wonder, and Miracles are in this WAVE.

Arise, shine; for thy light is come, and the glory of the Lord is risen upon thee. For, behold, the darkness shall cover the earth, and gross darkness the people: but the Lord shall arise upon thee, and his glory shall be seen upon thee. And the Gentiles shall come to thy light, and kings to the brightness of thy rising. (Isaiah 60:1-3 KJV

For the earth shall be filled with the knowledge of the glory of the Lord, as the waters cover the sea. Habakkuk 2:14 KJV

2017

THE PRESENTATION

Lo, I come. The Bridegroom cometh. He has been ready and waiting. Are you ready? For many must be purged and cleansed for presentation. This presentation is like no other. It involves much seen and unseen, visible and invisible in the heart. It is time. I have waited long enough. Prepare yourselves for visitation and encounters like no other time in your life. I will come with INCREASE.

Take my hand now as I have extended it to you. My touch will bring you into a new place of intimacy. This intimacy has no limits or boundaries. It is unlike your earthly concept. The minute you take my hand, the elevation will begin to become one. The presentation is an upgrade to walk with me in a new place. I Am longing for the touch. Are you? Come. Come now. Quickly!

Feel the rush of the winds of expectation all around you moving you suddenly into the prepared place. The excitement. All of heaven rejoices with each step you take. Come, Come now. Come quickly. The doors are open. Walk through with me into the prepared place.

The room is filled with the unspeakable. Take your seat now as I adore and adorn you. My love, my child. It is I who present you. No one else can. Rest in me. You are adored and adorned.

"As the hart panteth after the water brooks, so panteth my soul after thee, O God. My soul thirsteth for God, for the living God: when shall I come and appear before God?"
Psalm 42:1-2 KJV

"My beloved spake, and said unto me, Rise up, my love, my fair one, and come away."
Song of Solomon 2:10 KJV

"Then I said, Behold, here I am, coming to do Your will, O God, to fulfill what is written of Me in the volume of the Book."

Hebrews 10:7 AMPC

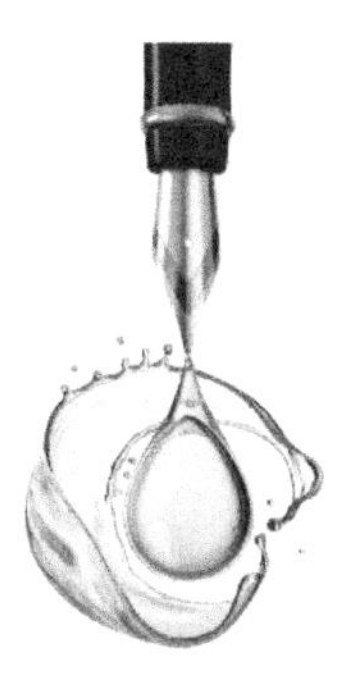

2017

THE BEAT

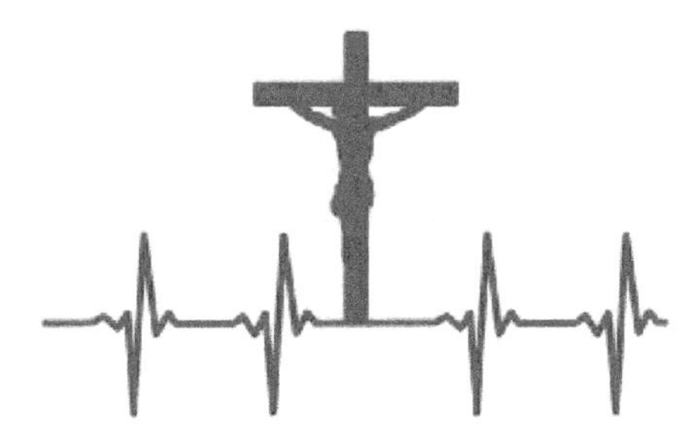

Hear the beat of my heart, my children. My heart beats for you. For **I AM** the many breasted one, El Shaddai. My heart beats for you. You can only hear it when you rest on me and rest in me. For **I AM** calling you to rest and see. Rest now. Cease from your labors. Rest and you will see the wonder of my GLORY.

For **I AM** the God to be discovered. To discover me is to know me and this is my desire. For many of my children do not really know me. I know you, your thoughts, your desires, and your fears. I know you. I made you. There are things about yourself that you have yet to discover. You will only discover them when you come to me. Come aside now and feel, come aside and hear my heart beat for you.

Desire me with all your heart NOW. For there is much to be discovered and it will only be discovered through the beat. The rhythm of the universe awaits your discovery.

And because ye are sons, God hath sent forth the Spirit of his Son into your hearts, crying, Abba, Father.
Galatians 4:6 KJV

The Lord is good, a Strength and Stronghold in the day of trouble; He knows, recognizes, has knowledge of, and understands those who take refuge and trust in Him.
Nahum 1:7 AMPC

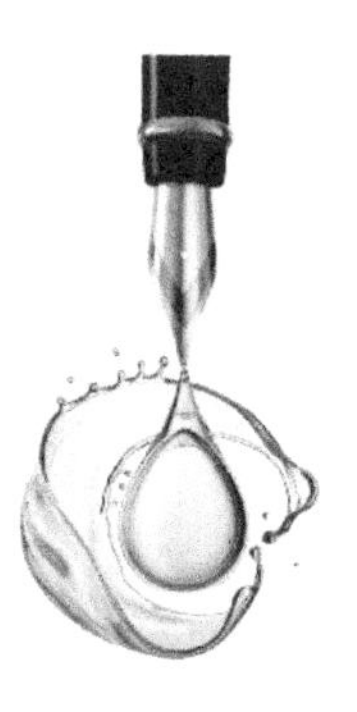

2017

AGREE WITH ME

These are the days that I need my people to be and walk in agreement with me. For are we not in a covenant? A covenant of blood shed by my precious Son. I will fulfill every word that has been spoken unto you. Look now.

It has begun and it is appearing before your very eyes. Look to me and see all that you need. It is coming. It is coming to pass. Yes, many are full of my glory and it is time to release that which I have imparted and planted within you. For I have reserved you for such a time as this. You were hidden for my special purpose. Awaken, Awaken and Arise now. It is the command. It is time to walk with me and be seen so that my glory will be displayed on earth for many to see.

As you walk with me, agree with me. Let me lead you to that which is unknown, the mysteries that I have reserved to be revealed. Chosen. Many were called but a few were Chosen, but they did not agree with me. Agree with me for it all. Agree with me for everything. Do I not see and know the place of your heart? I know when you are weak and strong. You receive strength from me. I will strengthen you now more than ever before. Agree with me. I am the source of all you need and I will provide. Did I not give you the air to breathe?

Watch and listen for the fresh wind that will usher you. It will usher you into the prepared place. When you agree with my Word, you agree with me, for I Am my Word. The Word walks in you and through you, Agree with me and see it all. Agree with me for the manifestation.

There is a place, a point in time when signs, miracles and wonders will unfold. That time is Now, but you must agree with me. I need you to agree with me so that heaven can touch the earth. I Am ready to rain down much that has never been seen. I need you to agree with me. Become my vessel completely and totally. Empty out the old. Shall I fill you over and over again? There shall be an overflow. You will feel my presence like never before. But you must agree with me. When you say, "Yes Lord," I will be there in way you have never known.

Take my hand and walk with me. Walk with me. You have to agree with me to walk into this new place. See it ahead. Take my hand now and I will lead you. Let us enter in. Come Now. Come Now. Come Now and stand beside me. Agree with me for your destiny. It is already written.

"Can two walk together, except they be agreed?"
Amos 3:3 KJV

"In the beginning was the Word, and the Word was with God, and the Word was God."
John 1:1

"Verily, verily, I say unto you, He that believeth on me, the works that I do shall he do also; and greater works than these shall he do; because I go unto my Father."
John14:12 KJV

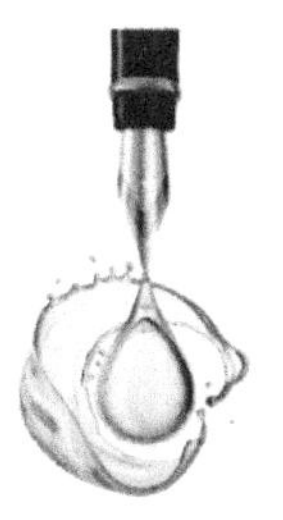

2017

VISION & SIGHT

My people are not seeing as I would have them to see. They only see the natural, that which the enemy puts before them. I desire that they see as I see. I Am their God and they should see as I see. It is MY vision that should be accelerated in the earth NOW. Watch and see.

For the doubters shall see. For the lukewarm shall see. Those on the fence shall see. They all shall see the wonder of my glory as it fill the earth. Many will have advance notice of my signs, wonders, and miracles as the call them. It is on the invasion of my will on the earth. I hear the cries of my people. I Am coming for all to see.

Many unexplained wonders are occurring now and will increase. Increase. Increase in areas that have not been known to man but to me. For I AM the LORD GOD ALMIGHTY and I do as I please in the heavens, the earth and the seas. What shall I say to MY people? Watch and see.

Those that know ME, those that wear MY seal, shall see and know the NEW. Much has been released and fall from the heavens NOW! You must be in position to receive it and them. I have opened the gates. Which gates? That is for you to see.

Lift your eyes NOW and SEE and you will SEE the gate. And that is the gate that you must come through. Come Through. COME THROUGH NOW! SEE NOW with NEW VISION. As you SEE it with MY vision, you shall SEE it with your sight.

Heaven's vision will become the earth's sight. The in the spirit shall see. Scales are being removed now as you read. Read MY WORD and SEE the NEW. Each WORD is designed to bring NEW revelation as you read. This time you shall SEE what has never been seen and you shall think what you never thought which shall clear your mind of doubt and unbelief. MY WORD will become more tangible now as you SEE.

Come up, come up higher so that you can SEE the wonder of my glory. I AM waiting. Take my hand and come up now. I AM restoring your original sight when you were fist with me. Nothing seemed impossible. The enemy of time has sought to displace and discourage you.

But know that I AM here and I AM above time for I AM the one who created time and all that is seen. There is much to be seen, and much to be known, and it is coming now as I have hastened to perform MY WORD in the lives of MY people, so that there will be no more wondering.

I AM taking wonder out and replacing with wonders. And they shall SEE and know and the shadow of doubt will be removed. Do not wonder how. Do not wonder why. Do not wonder. Just know it is the GREAT I AM who is the **WONDER.** It is written so SEE the vision. The books are opened and released. See the truth. See your truth as I AM coming to you NOW.

"I will stand at my guard post
And station myself on the tower;
And I will keep watch to see what He will say to me,
And what answer I will give as His spokesman when I am reproved."
Habakkuk 2:1 AMP

"For the earth shall be filled with the knowledge of the glory of the LORD, as the waters cover the sea."
Habakkuk 2:14 KJV

"Then said the LORD unto me, Thou hast well seen: for I will hasten my word to perform it.
Jeremiah 1:12 KJV

"This is the Lord's doing; it is marvellous in our eyes."
Psalm 118:23 KJV

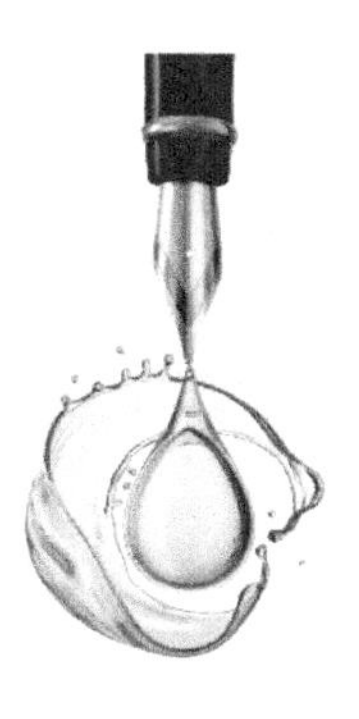

2018

HEAVEN'S CONDUIT

There are many vessels who have been called for me to flow through. I have called and called for them to come up higher. It is in that place that they will see. For I have called them to show them great and mighty things that I have planned of the earth. It is my plan. And it will work because I have created it. It is for my glory. **MY GLORY** will be revealed. **MY GLORY** will be revealed. **MY GLORY** will be released.

Now concerning Heaven's Conduit, I am lining up several of my vessels. They will be used mightily in the days to come. Many will be in ***AWE*** of who I will be using, but I know the heart of man. It is who **I** choose,

the one with the heart like David, that **I** will anoint. This anointing shall not come through man's hands, but directly from **ME**. It will flow directly from **ME**. It will be **MY** touch. And they shall know that it is **ME**. The flow will be intense, undeniable and notable. Many will be confused by who **I** choose. But it
Is **MY** choice. **I** choose the least among you. **HIDDEN**. They have been hidden for such a time as this.

Their names are being called and read in heaven. **LISTEN. LISTEN for your name**. Are you one of the ones? Do you desire to do the work for me? **LISTEN for MY whisper**. I will even give you sight and insight. Hear and obey in **MY** timing, not yours and you will see the wonders of my glory. When I speak, the portals of heaven are open for the flow of my power. It is your obedience to my voice. Listen and do not be distracted. **LISTEN. LISTEN. LISTEN for MY whisper.**

"For many are called, but few are chosen."
Matthew 22:14 KJV

"So then after the Lord had spoken unto them, he was received up into heaven, and sat on the right hand of God. And they went forth, and preached every where, the Lord working with them, and

confirming the word with signs following. Amen."
Mark 16:19-20 KJV

"But you are a chosen race, a royal priesthood, a dedicated nation, God's own purchased, special people, that you may set forth the wonderful deeds and display the virtues and perfections of Him Who called you out of darkness into His marvelous light."
1 Peter 2:9 AMPC

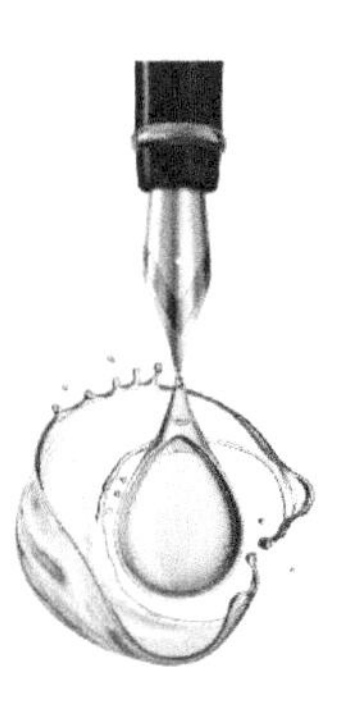

2018

THE PECULIAR

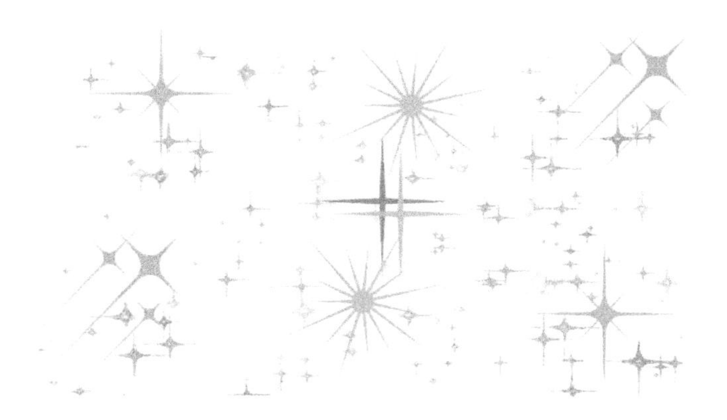

The PECULIAR are emerging. They are coming forth now from the highway and by ways. I have called them out. I have released a sound that they will to come. It is the sound of MY voice that moves them. They are on the March, moving to the forefront.

Emerging as stars, they will shine brightly for Me. There is a release, a Great Release. For I cause it to happen when I say it will happen. It is not up to man, but Me. It is My time. I, who sit in eternity, sees all. It will be a wonder to many, but not the Peculiar because that have been prepared and are waiting.

The sound of My voice moves them forward. It is an inner knowing. It is My voice. Awaken and Arise, for I have sounded the alarm. It is My voice that is the alarm and My voice alone. Wake up now and see the wonder of My glory among those many thought that I would not use. Theirs is a different hunger. Many will say where did they come from? From the chambers of the Most High. See My glory upon them. They come to display My glory and My glory alone because I can trust them.

And the words of their mouth will make the nations shake. And the words of their mouths. And the words of their mouths. And the words of their mouth are My Words indeed. And the word of their mouths. And the words of their mouths are filled with oil and honey. Filled to the overflow. And the words of their mouths. And the words of their mouths. And the words of their mouth I command so shall they speak.

I command so shall they speak. The atmosphere is Mine by the words that they will speak. For it is time, and it shall be SUDDENLY. See the atmosphere is filled with the words of SUDDENLY. And the words of their mouths are mine. Purge to emerge.

"Arise, shine; for thy light is come, and the glory of the Lord is risen upon thee.
(Isaiah 60:1

"The sheep that are My own hear and are listening to My voice; and I know them, and they follow Me. And I give them eternal life, and they shall never lose it or perish throughout the ages. To all eternity they shall never by any means be destroyed. And no one is able to snatch them out of My hand."
John 10:27-28 AMPC

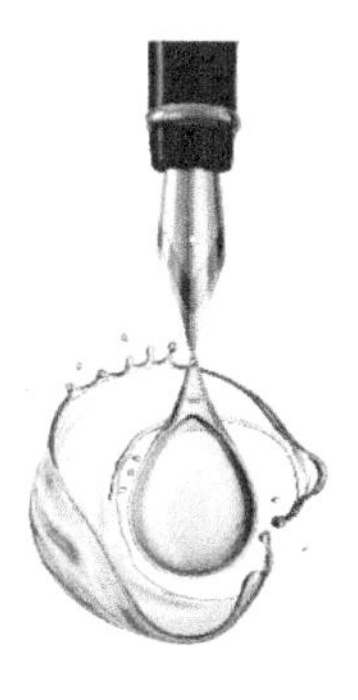

2018

THE PERPETUAL WHISPER

I Am always speaking. Are you listening? I speak in ways that you know not of but you must be in communion with me to hear. You want to know what is on my mind and my heart, spend time with me. For my time is not your time. Come when I call in the whisper.

You will awaken in the night. It is I who awaken you with my whisper. Distractions keep you from My whisper. Fine tune your ears to my frequency. My voice goes deeper than you know. LISTEN. LISTEN now for the whisper. It will direct your path. You know My voice. Do not be distracted. The enemy comes to steal from you when I whisper. Be on guard and focus. Focus on Me and My whisper.

I Am calling many to the reserved place that has been set before the foundation of the world. Understand that My time is not like your time, the time that I created. For I am the Creator of time. Hear My whisper, but Hear My Roar over you My child, My breath is in My whisper and My breath is in My Roar. I will whisper over you, for you are Mine. Even My whisper to you is a roar to the enemy. Whether it is a whisper or a roar you will hear and know that I Am with you.

The sheep that are My own hear and are listening to My voice; and I know them, and they follow Me.
John 10:27 AMPC

A sower went out to sow his seed: and as he sowed, some fell by the way side; and it was trodden down, and the fowls of the air devoured it. And some fell upon a rock; and as soon as it was sprung up, it withered away, because it lacked moisture. And some fell among thorns; and the thorns sprang up with it, and choked it. And other fell on good ground, and sprang up, and bare fruit an hundredfold. And when he had said these things, he cried, He that hath ears to hear, let him hear. And his disciples asked him, saying, What might this parable be? And he said, Unto you it is given to know the mysteries of the kingdom of God: but to others in parables; that seeing they might not see, and hearing

they might not understand. Now the parable is this: The seed is the word of God. Those by the way side are they that hear; then cometh the devil, and taketh away the word out of their hearts,
lest they should believe and be saved.
Luke 8:5-12

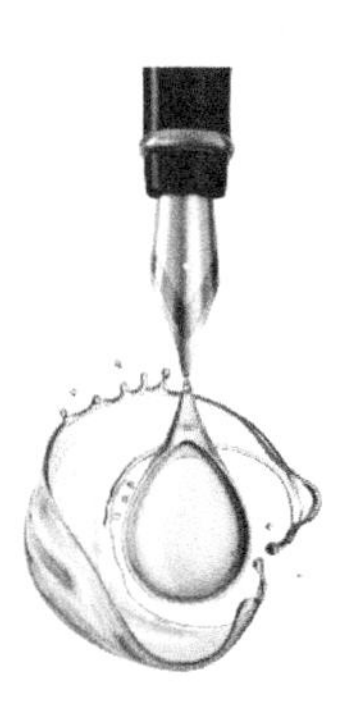

2018

IT IS ACTIVATION TIME

I will activate that which you do not know about and did not expect. It has been hidden. Watch My timing, unveiling My plan, My purpose is greater that you can imagine. I will give you an anointing that you did not know about. It will be activated by me and not by man because there has never been this type of encounter. ATMOSPHERES, ATMOSPHERES……………………..

"For my thoughts are not your thoughts, neither are your ways my ways, saith the LORD. For as the heavens are higher than the earth, so are my ways higher than your ways, and my thoughts than your thoughts." Isaiah 55:8-9

"For it was so, when Jezebel cut off the prophets of the LORD, that Obadiah took an hundred prophets, and hid them by fifty in a cave, and fed them with bread and water." I Kings 18:4 KJV

"God standeth in the congregation of the mighty; he judgeth among the gods. How long will ye judge unjustly, and accept the persons of the wicked? Selah." Psalm 82:1-3 KJV

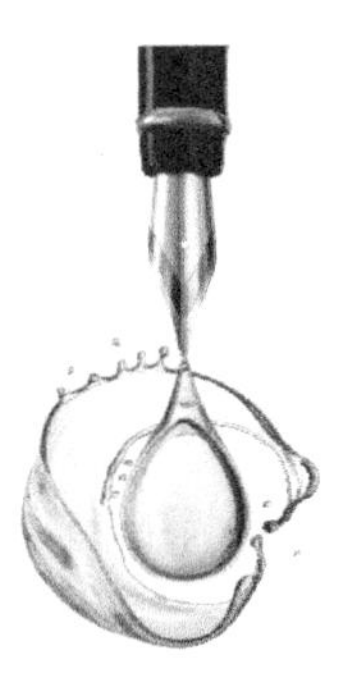

2018

INSTRUMENTS OF VALOR

My instruments, My people shall come forth NOW like never before with demonstrations and manifestations of My power. They all have been chosen from the foundation of the world. Equipped, Empowered and Encapsulated with My DNA. The forces of hell will not be able to stop these few, yes few. Not everyone is called to operate in this realm.

Remember the spiritual giants of old. They sought after me with all their heart, mind, and soul. They desired Me and only Me, to be in My presence. Who will come? Who will come and stay? Who will come and lay before Me? Is it you? Can you lay it all down for Me?

Now is the time to seek Me like never before. Yes, you have been seeking Me, but now it is time to seek Me in a NEW way. For I AM the God of the NEW to you but old to Me. I did it all in eternity and released it into time for you.

Now, know that the weapons of warfare are mighty through Me, through Me alone will you win. Through me alone will you save. Through me alone will the enemy flee. It is through me alone.

I AM changing the rank of some of My Kingdom people. You must have a Kingdom mindset. It is Kingdom. I AM Kingdom.

Ready Riders shall prevail. Prepare yourself for the coming of My glory. There is an opening. I AM the opening. I AM the way. I AM the truth. I AM the life and I give it abundantly. Open your eyes. Lift your eyes. For I have given you sight beyond sight to see the victory that awaits you. It is already done. They will marvel in awe at the power of their God flowing through you. For you will even be in wonder. For I have chosen you to be an instrument of valor so that the world will know that I AM the God whom you serve and live and have your being.

"The angel of the Lord appeared unto him, and said unto him, The Lord is with thee, though mighty man of valour." Judges 6:12

"For many are called, but few are chosen.
Matthew 22:14
"And these signs shall follow them that believe; In my name shall they cast out devils; they shall speak with new tongues they shall serpents; and if they drink any deadly thing, it shall not hurt them; they shall lay hands on the sick, and they shall recover."
Mark 16:17-19

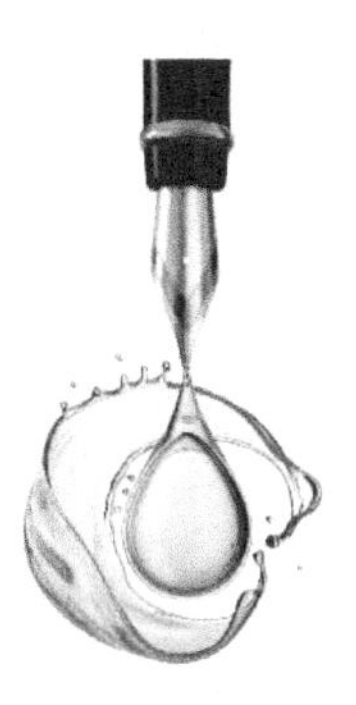

2018

MY BLOOD SPEAKS

Learn to use the power of My Blood for **IT STILL SPEAKS**. It makes a Sound in the realm of the Spirit. A Sound that shatters the plan of the enemy A Sound that destroys the enemy's devices against you. Learn to Speak the Sound of My Blood. Hear the Sound of what it does to the enemy. My Blood is All Powerful.

There is no blood like My Blood, the greatest sacrifice for All. It Speaks. It covers. It protects. It

Delivers. Can you see the Power of My Blood in your life? It will and It can deliver you from Anything.

Even as you read these words, I Am delivering you. Deliverance in your mind and in your thoughts. All it took was one drop of My Blood to change Everything in Your Life. Do You Believe? Do You Believe My Sacrifice for YOU? I was slain just for You to **BELIEVE**. **BELIEVE** My Love for You.

I Am and have always been right there with You. In Communion, You do this in remembrance of Me. Remember the Sacrifice. Remember the Power of the Sacrifice. My Love for You is Limitless, Boundless, and Eternal. Who else would pay such a price for LOVE? Seek Me and Hear Me like never before. I Stand and I Wait for You to **COME CLOSER.**

"What have you done? Listen! I can hear the voice of your brother's blood crying out to Me from the ground!"
Genesis 4:10 AMP

He went once for all into the Holy of Holies of heaven, not by virtue of the blood of goats and calves[by which to make reconciliation between God and man, but His

own blood, having found and secured a complete redemption, an everlasting release for us. For if [the mere] sprinkling of unholy and defiled persons with blood of goats and bulls and with the ashes of a burnt heifer is sufficient for the purification of the body, How much more surely shall the blood of Christ, Who by virtue of His eternal Spirit, His own preexistent divine personality has offered Himself as an unblemished sacrifice to God, purify our consciences from dead works and lifeless observances to serve the ever living God?

Hebrews 9:12-14 AMPC

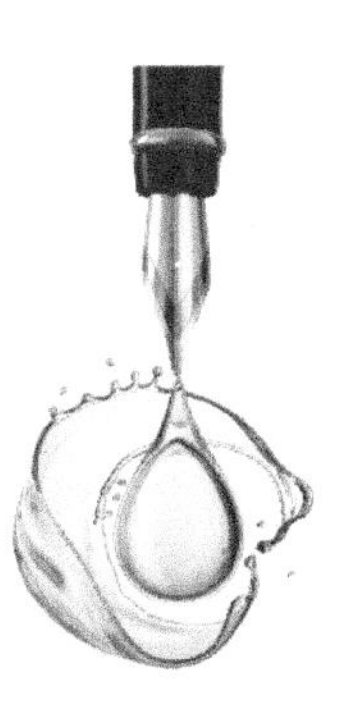

2019

HE HAS TURNED THE PAGE

I Am the One who turns the page on the Books of Life. I turn the page when I will. It is all in My timing. Many pages are turning as I fast forward you in to the Prepared Place. See and know that I turn the pages of your life quickly. You will feel the quickness coming upon you in the breeze of My wind. My wind is blowing now even as you read these words, there is a breeze.

The breeze feels like a breeze, but it is a violent wind. You asked what is the wind. Now I will show you and you will see all that I have for such a time as this. You will thank me for turning the page in My time not yours. For I know all things about your, about your time, about your life. I see and know because I Am the One who created you.

I Am revealing the hidden Now, that which has been kept back for the ages. I Am the Revelator. I Am the One who interrupts time with the divine. I can do it if you Believe it. Divine interruptions are My specialty. To you they are miracles because your mind cannot conceive that which is out of the ordinary. Exposure to the Supernatural will become natural to you. But you must Believe. Look to me for the extraordinary and it will become natural to you.

Do not be limited in your thinking. It limits your ability to conceive the Supernatural. My thoughts are not natural as I Am not natural. Prepare your mind to receive My thoughts, the ones that you can handle and conceive. It is time for My thoughts to be manifested in the earth. Where are My carriers? I need carriers of My thoughts. They will be able to conceive and achieve the manifestation of My desires.

What was in the past is in the past. For it is a new day. Do you not expect me to do a new thing? It is already done. You only have to see it and know it by

Faith. The Faith that I have given unto you. You want to know what was in the wind. Flames and Fire and Passion for Me. I have ignited many. Those who have been ignited, their page has turned and turned and turned. There is a turning in their spirit. It is hotter than ever before and it will continue to ignite. It will burn fervently, hot with desire for My glory to come in ways unprecedented. It is time to see that which has never been seen.

I turn the pages in the Eternal realm and it manifests in your belief, your faith in the natural. Believe Me Now. Believe that I have turned the pages of your life. Not just one, but as many as I have chosen. Your placement, your arrival at the designated place is imminent. I Am sending the wind to usher you in. The doors are open to the place I have prepared for you. Come. Come Now.

Your eyes saw my unformed substance, and in Your book all the days [of my life] were written before ever they took shape, when as yet there was none of them. Psalm 139:16 AMPC

Like an open book, you watched me grow from conception to birth; all the stages of my life were spread out before you, The days of my life all prepared before I'd even lived one day. MSG

For He foreordained us, destined us, planned in love for us to be adopted, revealed as His own children through Jesus Christ, in accordance with the purpose of His will because it pleased Him and was His kind intent.
Ephesians 1:5 AMPC

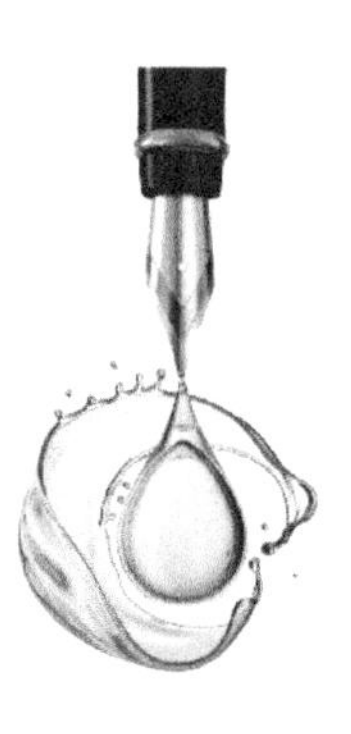

2019

A PIECE OF ME

A piece of Me is inside of every Believer. It is called Faith. I have blessed you with a piece of me. For I Am the One who gives you the Faith to operate and move in the natural realm. As I am Spirit, Faith is Spirit. You have the deposit so be fruitful and multiply. Your Faith is a key. Use it to access that which is waiting for you.

Let Faith, the piece of me permeate everything that you do and say. For now is the time when many things will come to pass. Things that you may have forgotten about, but they are coming. Keep your Faith intact. Believe me for the impossible. Am I not a God who is right there with you? Is there anything too hard for Me?

I loved you enough to send My Son. I gave you Him, I gave you My Holy Spirit, and I gave you My Faith. They are all a piece of Me. For lo, I Am with you through all time, to the end of time, because you have a piece of Me. I give you a piece of Me to operate like Me.

For by the grace of God given to me I say to everyone of you not to think more highly of himself and of his importance and ability than he ought to think; but to think so as to have sound judgment, as God has apportioned to each a degree of faith and a purpose designed for service.
Romans 12:3 AMP

Because of the grace allotted to me, I can respectfully tell you not to think of yourselves as being more important than you are; devote your minds to sound judgment since God has assigned to each of us a measure of faith. Voice

Nevertheless when the Son of man cometh, shall he find faith on the earth?
Luke 18:8 KJV

But here's the question: when the Son of Man comes, will He find anyone who still has faith? Voice

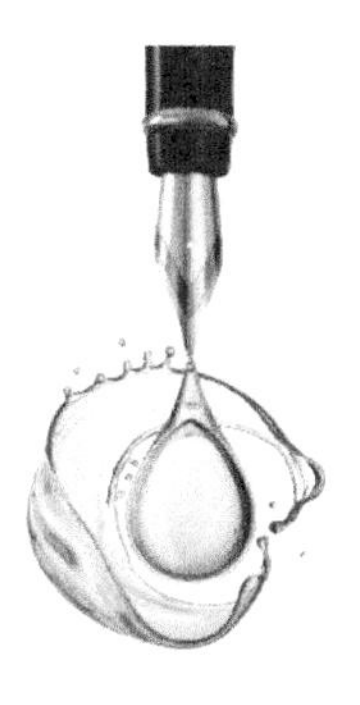

2019

THE DATE OF APPLICATION

The day you hear my voice, harden not your heart. My voice thunders as mighty waters, breaks through. There is a breaking. Apply what you hear, even in the still small voice, even in a whisper.

The time is NOW to move because I Am speaking. Hear now. Hear now and move. For I Am moving. What move should I say? You know that I Am with you. I have never left you or forsaken you. See ME. Hear ME. Feel ME. For I Am ever present and you are in My presence. I created you to worship ME, to praise ME. So do not allow anyone or anything to hinder or stop you from coming deeper into my presence.

My Word is forever settled in heaven. My Word, not the word of a man, but My Word. Who can come against My Word. It does not come back to Me void. For I watch over My Word for its performance. It performs. It performs on the day, the time that you hear it. That is the Date of Your Application for it is an appointed time. It is the time that I have chosen to display My Power, My Glory in the earth through you. Have you applied My Word to your life? To your situation?

Apply My Word and you SHALL SEE. Apply My Word NOW on the day that you hear My Voice and it will manifest. All of heaven is waiting on you. Trust Me. Trust Me to bring you through and bring you out. Rest In Me. In My Voice is My Promise, which is Yes and Amen.

"The sheep that are My own hear and are listening to My voice; and I know them, and they follow Me."

John 10:27 KJV

Remember what it says: "Today when you hear his voice, don't harden your hearts as Israel did when they rebelled."
Hebrews 3:15 NLT

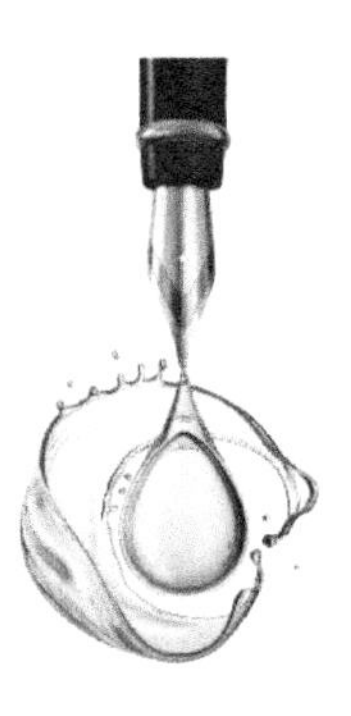

2019

THE GIFT OF THE GREATER

It is My Gift to you that no one else can give unto you. It will not be found on the earth until I release it through you. Many are waiting for this to manifest. Keys will be released for the activation now.

Prepare yourself for the Greater. The Gift is already in you. There was never a deposit, but a forming. I formed you with the Greater before I released you into the earth realm. You have it but it is only I who can activate it because it is for My purpose. The purpose is to give Me the glory as I Am the Creator of everything that exists.

I have been waiting until this appointed time for My people to be in a place for the Gift of the Greater to come forth. It is coming forth now! It is coming forth now! Look, See, Expect, and Anticipate the Greater manifestation of My presence, My glory not only moving in the earth, but in you and through you.

For the time has come and it is now even as you read these words the seed is going forth and it is now. The Gift of the Greater is now. Look and see and know that the Greater One is in you! Am I not the Great God? I there anything too hard for Me? If I said it, I will do it and I will make it good for you! I Am waiting. Just trust me! Trust Me and See. The Greater is My Greatness. It is My Gift.

Little children, you are of God you belong to Him and have already defeated and overcome them [the agents of the antichrist], because He Who lives in you is greater, mightier than he who is in the world.
1 John 4:4

Behold, I am the LORD, the God of all flesh: is there any thing too hard for me? Jeremiah 32:27

Praise God for this incredible, unbelievable, indescribable gift!
2 Corinthians 9:15

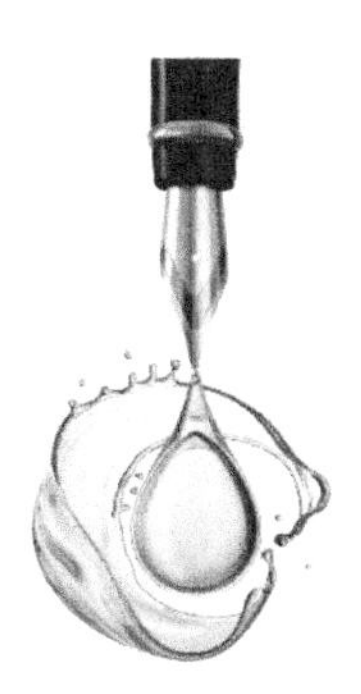

2019

THE PATTERN OF THOUGHT

Every time I have given someone a thought, I Am using that vessel, that mind to produce My purpose in the earth. I have many thoughts to give to My people, My vessels, but their minds are not ready. For they concentrate on the natural realm on the impossible, but with Me all things are possible. Their minds must be ready to receive in order to conceive in their heart and then proceed to produce. It all comes from Me. Everything that you see, who else but Me. For I Am the Creator of everything seen and unseen.

Now is the time for the thoughts of My chosen vessels to change. No longer will they think as the world thinks. They will not be hindered by the old thought patterns because I Am creating the NEW within them.

There has always been a battle for the mind of My People, My Believers. The contention is for the ability to create that, which comes from My thoughts. It is time for My thoughts to be prevalent in the earth. Tell the people to get their minds ready for that which has been thought to be impossible is coming and that shall see it with their very eyes.

Many will be struck with amazement for that which they have been believing for all this time shall come forth. Breakthrough. There is a Breaking Forth into the earth. Believe and See. For My glory shall fill the earth. Believe and See. Know that I Am with you, but you must believe to see what I Am doing at this time.

Your mind is the gateway to the miracles that shall come forth. Get your mind ready to receive and you heart ready to conceive. For I have said that My thoughts are not your thoughts, and My ways are not your ways. Seek Me and you will find Me. Acknowledge Me in all your ways for I Am with you.

Prepare to receive the divine ideas that will

distinguish you because I Am your GOD. They will be proven and many will See that I Am REAL.

Everything begins with a thought. My thoughts give way to perception of insight to revelation of mysteries. The atmosphere is full with thoughts, but what are they producing? Now is the time for the thoughts that produce My Glory in the earth.

I am calling those who can carry My thoughts and produce for the Kingdom. You must be prepared for the supernatural. It is that time, the time of DISTINGUISHING My Kingdom, My People.

What are you thinking now? Will it determine your future? Let Me have your mind and you will see the wonder and the beauty of My glory in your life. It is time to think differently.

I Am preparing My people's mind for the capacity for that which they will carry for the future. Tell them to prepare their minds NOW. For I Am enlarging their territory. This time is about your thoughts and what you carry for My Glory. Carry it well for the manifestation will surely come. Prepare your mind to receive the Greater. It is all about your Capacity Now.

KINGDOM THOUGHTS EXPAND HIS VISION EXPONENTIALLY.

That, regarding your previous way of life, you put off your old self, completely discard your former nature, which is being corrupted through deceitful desires, and be continually renewed in the spirit of your mind having a fresh, untarnished mental and spiritual attitude.
Ephesians 4:22-23 AMPC

The counsel of the Lord stands forever, the thoughts of His heart through all generations.
Psalm 33:11 AMPC

"I don't think the way you think. The way you work isn't the way I work." God's Decree.
Isaiah 55:8 MSG

Your works are marvelous, O Eternal One. Your thoughts are unfathomable.
Psalm 92:5

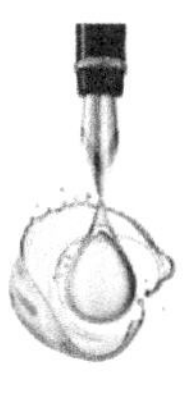

2019

EXTRAORDINARY COMMUNICATION

Every time I pray in the spirit, I connect with the Spirit of God in the language that is not earthly, but the language of the country, that many lack understanding. But, the Holy Spirit provides translation. He communicates the words that the Father speaks. His messages are pure and undefiled directing the way that I should go.

Wisdom, revelation and understanding to certain truth are contained in this communication. Plans for the future that are already established, in the spirit are released to those who can carry them for the fulfillment of His purpose.

On the first day of the New Year 5780. I received the following words in prayer. I perceive that this is the beginning of something new in the composition of writing, an upgrade in this New Era.

It is time for many of My people to communicate on a different frequency. It is a gift that I give. You Believe in Me, Believe in My gift. For it is freely given. Seek Me and come farther than your natural language. It is the tongues of distinction. It distinguishes you from the ordinary because it is Me praying in you and through you. Come beyond what you know. It is My expression through you. Come, Come up higher. Come, Come beyond the limits of your mind. Come, Come and see. Come, Come and hear.

For I speak to you in your language. Speak to Me in mine and I will give the interpretation. For it is a New Time and a New Era. I will Flood and Flow My people with signs and wonders unimaginable to you but not to Me. Check your imagination. What you can see, you can be.

Speak Now and see, for I Am coming like never before. The scribe will write My Word that will have fire for the eyes that see them and hear My voice as it is read. Yes, yes, Now is the time, it will do the work and that should see and Believe. Watch Me perform My word in the lives of many as a demonstration of power for those who are on assignment. New assignments are being given out. Acceleration, Elevation Advancement. All for the Kingdom purpose. Advance Now. Go forth and conquer the land. The Word is nigh thee, in thy mouth. Speak it and see the display of my glory in the earth moving as a mighty wave as a tsunami flowing among you and through you.

Communicate with me now in the New. Do not limit My voice. Don't limit your voice. Open your mouth and I will fill it and I will speak. Become the Speaking Spirit that I have called you to be. The time is Now. Now is the Time. It Is My time.

And these signs will follow those who believe: they will be able to cast out demons in My name, speak with new tongues.
Mark 16:17 Voice

Thus tongues are a sign not for believers but for unbelievers, while prophecy is not for unbelievers but for believers.

1 Corinthian 14:22 CJB
If I speak with the tongues of men and of angels, but have not love for others growing out of God's love for me, then I have become only a noisy gong or a clanging cymbal just an annoying distraction.
1 Corinthians 13:1 AMP

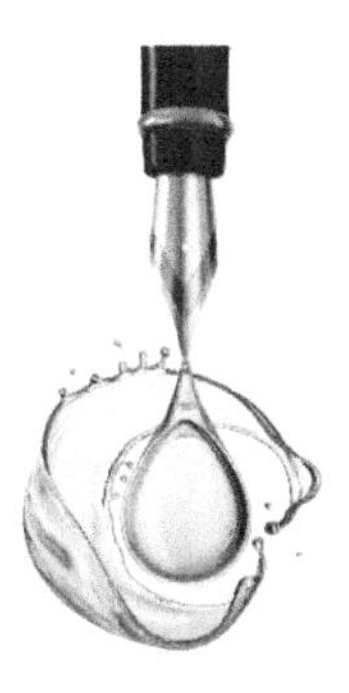

2019

LIMITATIONS

Nothing ever remains the same. It is your perception. It is a New Day. Can you even imagine what has been done while you sleep? It is already done. It has been done since before creation. While you rest, there is work in My creation. Time limits your perception, but I Am Eternal and what it appears that I do has already been done. Think on that.

UNBELIEF has the word LIE within it. Stretch your mind. Stretch your imagination. That is why I gave it to you. So go beyond the LIE of the enemy through unbelief. Take the brakes off. Take the limits off. If you can conceive then it can be achieved. I do not LIMIT you. Your mind LIMITS you. How do you think that you get the innovative, the inventions? It is through the seed of a thought. Clear the runway of you mind. For what I Am about to do through you, you would have never imagined. What you imagine is only a drop in the bucket.

Do NOT LIMIT Me! I desire to do more than you know. Do NOT LIMIT Me! When you LIMIT Me, you LIMIT My power. You LIMIT the witness of My truth, my existence for all to see. Continue to give Me the glory in all that you do for others to see who I really am, the Lover of your soul.

For I Am a good God and I love My people. Yes, My people. I know them all. I know each and every one and even those to come. I wait patiently for their arrival. They are coming and you will see the glory of the Lord in the land of the living. My houses and My Kingdom will be filled to the overflow.

Change your perception of who I Am and you will see. It is in the intimacy with me. For I love you with an everlasting love. I loved you before you knew me. I loved you even when you that you understood Me and did not. It is simple. I Love You now and I will continue to love you for My Love is Eternal.

To know me is to know My Word. That is why it is written. My Word is My Voice. My Word is a Love Letter. Continue to seek Me and you shall find Me and what you will find in Me, through Me, and about Me is beyond your current comprehension. So renew your mind daily and do not LIMIT Me with your earthly thoughts. Think beyond what you see. Think beyond what you know. Get your mind ready. Take the LIMITS off.

The LORD looked down from heaven upon the children of men, to see if there were any that did understand, and seek God.
Psalm 14:2 KJV

The Eternal leans over from heaven to survey the sons of Adam. No one is missed, and no one can hide. He searches to see who understands true wisdom, who desires to know the True God.
Voice

I love those who love me, and those who seek me early and diligently shall find me.
Proverbs 8:17 AMPC

I will show my love to those who passionately love me. For they will search and search continually until they find me.
TPT

Again and again they limited God, preventing him from blessing them.
Continually they turned back from him
and provoked the Holy One of Israel!
Psalm 78:41 TPT

Your progress will have no limits when you come along with me, and you will never stumble as you walk along the way.
Proverbs 4:12 TPT

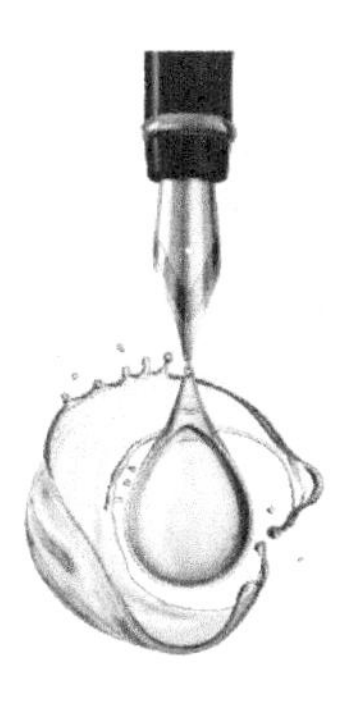

2019

THE SOUND OF HEAVEN

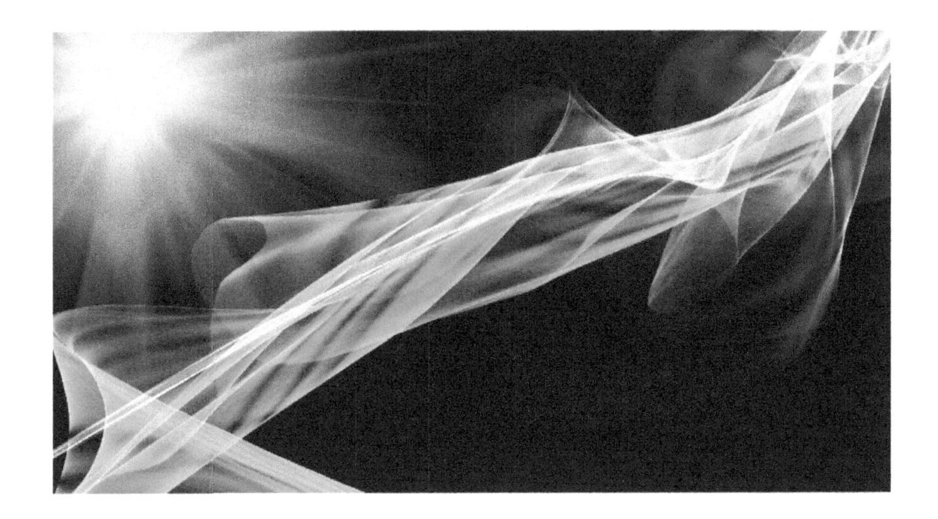

The Sound of heaven is not racial. It breaks all earthly barriers. He is looking for vessels to release the Sound. Hope is in the Sound. Love is in the Sound. Peace is in the Sound. I AM is in the Sound and I AM the Sound. I AM the Sound for all to hear.

Who can hear Me? Who can hear Me and make the Sound? The Sound that breaks all barriers, all fleshly barriers, all manmade barriers? Who? Where are you? Come to Me now and recieive The Assignment of My Sound. The Sound of My Glory is in My wind and it is blowing Now.Come Now. Come Close. For It is released.

The wind is blowing The Sound for those who will hear. I AM the God of Abraham, I AM the God of Isaac, I AM the God of Jacob, I AM the God of All United. I AM the God of Moses, I AM the God of David. I AM the God of ALL and ALL.

"A sound roars from the sky without warning, the roar of a violent wind, and the whole house where you are gathered reverberates with the sound."
Acts 2:2 The Voice

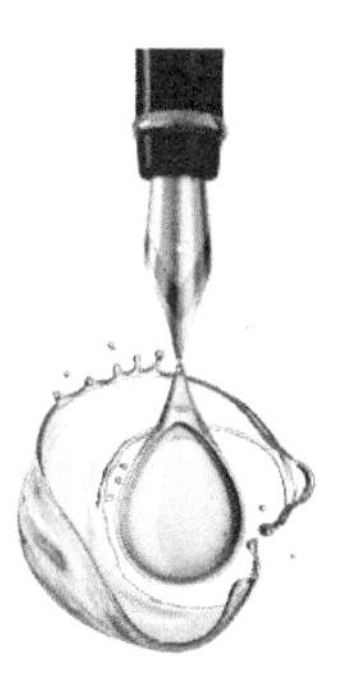

2019

THE POWER OF SPEAKING HIS NAME

The Power of Speaking His Name when we who Believe in the Power of His Name, atmospheres change in His name. His name and His Word. The forces of darkness recognize the Power spoken in a Believer who Believes in The Name. His Name, Jesus, stops time because the Name of the Creator has been spoken by the one who Believes in the Name. The supernatural Power of His Name. If you Believe in The Name, you Believe in the Power.

"I will worship toward Your holy temple and praise Your name for Your loving-kindness and for Your truth and faithfulness; for You have exalted above all else Your name and Your word* and *You have magnified Your word above all Your name!"

(Psalm 138:2 AMPC)

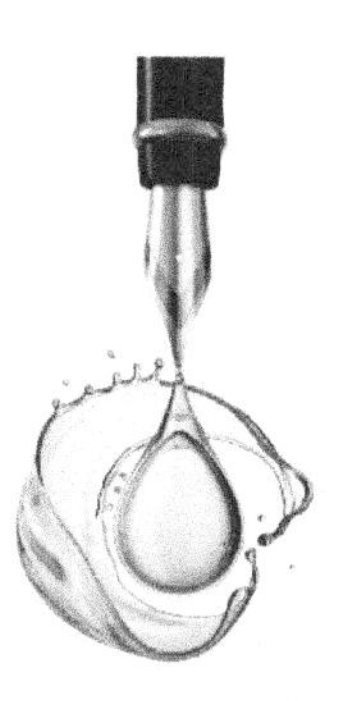

2019

THE SCENT OF THE LORD

Breathe In. Breathe Out. Breathe Deeply. Breathe In. Breathe Out. Breathe Deeply. Breathe Me In. Breathe Out every care, every worry. Everything that does not belong to you. Breathe Out that which I have not given you that which has been planted to derail you, to confuse you, to stop you, to hinder you. **BREATHE NOW! BREATHE NOW!**

For I cause My Breath to cover you, to fill you if you just BREATHE ME! BREATHE. BREATHE. My Breath is the Breath of Life. BREATHE. BREATHE more of ME. BREATHE. BREATHE. Continue to

Breathe Me and see. BREATHE. BREATHE. Always remember to BREATHE.

For I have Breathed on you in more ways that you know or see. My fragrance fill the atmosphere around you. Breathe Me In and live like no other time in your life. Breathe Me In. In My Breath is life and life abundantly. I came to give that to you.

BREATHE. BREATHE NOW and LIVE. Live for ME! For I AM soon to come, so BREATHE and Live. Live for ME! My hand is upon many that do not yet understand the weight of MY BREATH. For I Breathe life and it is the abundant life that they seek for and it is in ME. BREATHE. For I created the air that you breathe. BREATHE IN ME with each Breath. BREATHE IN ME. Today I say BREATHE.

"It is the Spirit of God that made me, which has stirred me up, and the breath of the Almighty that gives me life which inspires me."

Job 33:4 AMPC

But thanks be to God, Who in Christ always leads us in triumph as trophies of Christ's victory and through us

spreads and makes evident the fragrance of the knowledge of God everywhere."
2 Corinthians 2:14 AMPC

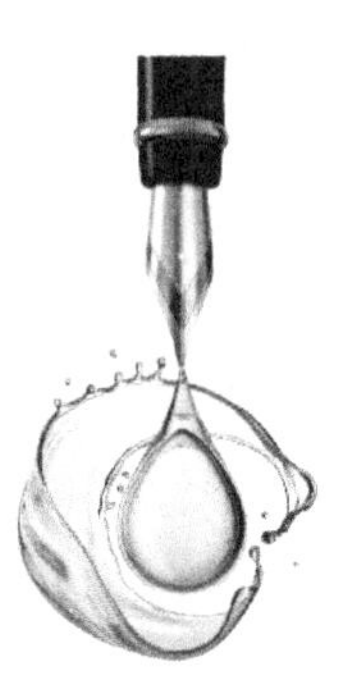

2019

A WELL WATERED GARDEN

I Am watering My people. They will be fruitful in every aspect of their lives. My people that have been hidden will come forth in such as a time as this. Their timing is by My hand and My grand design. Do not think that you will see and know who it is, for they are securely and secretly hidden. At the appointed time, I will remove the veil and reveal their identity.

They will be used to Rebuild and Restore My glory in the earth. The builders are coming with new bricks and mortar. It will not be the same. Everything has already been changed in the Spirit. Prepare to see it the natural. You see I already see it. But you are mistaken by the mirage. Your spirit will be prepared for your eyes to see what is to come. Stay connected to the Spirit for the deeper revelation.

I Am watering you with fresh spring of revelation. Drink now if you are thirsty. I will create a thirst in you that comes only to be quenched by My water. And new fruit shall spring forth from seeds that have long been planted. Many will taste of My goodness through you.

You are being watered as you read these words. The refreshing has begun and the outpouring to the overflow. Everywhere you look blessings, blessings, and more blessings. Here is the cup, drink to be refreshed. It is the living water that will flow through you and from you. I Am the Good Shepherd and I tend to you. I tend to My sheep. I know what they need and when it is needed. I Am the Good Shepherd and I tend to My sheep. Drink Now! Taste the sweetness of My Goodness. Drink Now! There is a rain that will also drench you, soak you. You are becoming a Well-Watered Garden.

And the Lord shall guide you continually and satisfy you in drought and in dry places and make strong your bones. And you shall be like a watered garden and like a spring of water whose waters fail not.
Isaiah 58:11 AMPC

You are like a tree, planted by flowing, cool streams of water that never run dry.
Your fruit ripens in its time; your leaves never fade or curl in the summer sun.
No matter what you do, you prosper.
Psalm 1:3 Voice

He who believes in Me, who cleaves to and trusts in and relies on Me as the Scripture has said, From his innermost being shall flow continuously springs and rivers of living water.
John 7:38 AMPC

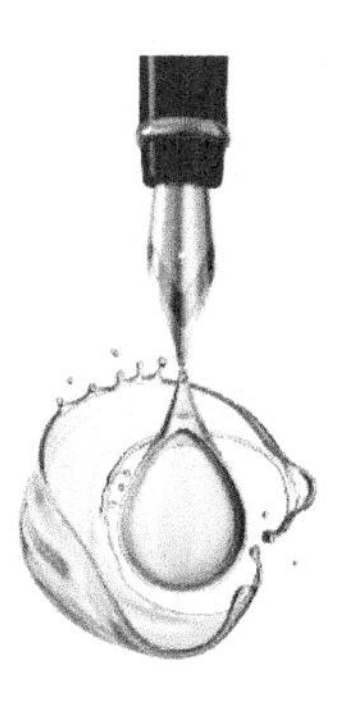

2020

OPEN SCROLLS

Many scrolls have been opened for this time to reveal My purpose in the lives of many. For they are now in the place as they stand before me that I can release My true purpose. Yes, they are open. I have broken the seal, that which has been sealed before time began. Who are these? They are the ones that many thought unusable by Me. For they are ferocious in their praise and worship. They roar the roar of the Lion of the tribe of Judah. The roar loud from the heart for Me.

My angels will now minister to them. I will not lose a generation that seeks me fervently. They are coming.

They are coming in great numbers. Do not reject them based on what is visible to your eye, but it is My eye that sees. I see what you cannot see unless I allow it. I hold their secrets, the secrets of their hearts. These secrets are the keys that will open the treasures that I have set in place. My goodness and mercy covers them and keeps them covered.

Now it will be seen who they really are and how I have preserved them for the Kingdom to do the great exploits. They see Me and know Me unlike any other. There is no comparison. There will be no comparison because I do something different as I please. Receive them. Accept them as My power flows through them.

It will be intense and fervent fire upon them and flow through them. Fire falls Now. The Fire falls. The fire. A fresh baptism for those who want it. It is in your desire. Desire Me. Desire Me Only and the fire will fall. Many do not know or understand what I am doing, but continue to seek Me and seek My face and I will reveal that which you need to sustain you and give you peace. Rest in Me. Trust in Me. Have I not said that I am with you always? It is all prepared just for you.

There is a season, a time appointed for everything and a time for every delight and event or purpose under heaven.
Ecclesiastes 3:1 AMP

This is the generation of them that seek him, that seek thy face, O Jacob. Selah.
Psalm 24:6;

When thou saidst, Seek ye my face; my heart said unto thee, Thy face, LORD, will I seek.

Psalm 27:8

But the people that do know their God shall be strong, and do exploits.
Daniel 11:32 KJV

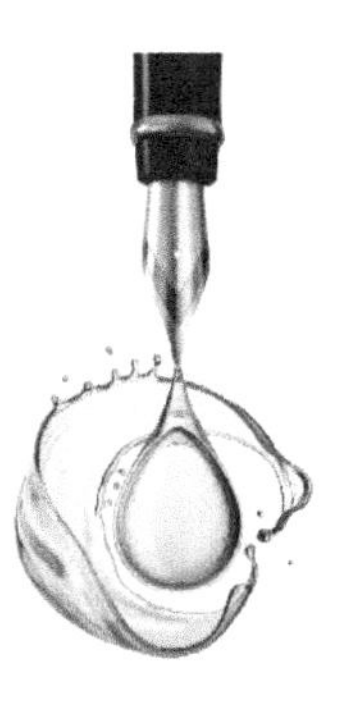

2020

TESTIMONY

Testimony is the old and new form of evangelism. What do you say about your GOD that fills the atmosphere? It is the display of His power on the earth in and through you. Redefining testimony. Everyone can give voice to the power of GOD and the atmosphere changes. The atmospheres hear that the Creator is doing it and reminding creation and who He is. Your faith and your words of HIS power causes atmospheric and revelatory changes in places that you cannot see. It causes a frequency to flow.

When you testify of the GOD that we serve, you are letting this world and the enemy know that HIS power is still in the earth flowing through those of us who BELIEVE.

There will be an anointing on the true testimonies from Me in the days to come, How I Am revealing Myself to those who do not know Me. The power of the words of My chosen vessels will be as mighty arrows charging and changing the atmosphere of UNBELIEF. The desperate will receive, the hungry will eat, and the thirsty will drink. Think it not strange the fiery trial that came to try you, it was about My glory, the weight of My glory, the heavyweights that would speak for Me.

Flood the atmosphere with the words of My goodness so that the clouds will form and move to rain the outpouring, the Showers of Blessings. Every time one of My Believers calls My name, the atmosphere is shaken all around them, even as they go. The Excellency of My name is revealed throughout all the earth. It Shall Be. And that is why your words matter. Say what I say and you will see what I see. Unto whom shall the Lord be revealed?

And they overcame him because of the blood of the Lamb, and because of the word of their testimony. Revelation 12:11a AMP

So that the genuineness of your faith may be tested, your faith which is infinitely more precious than the perishable gold which is tested and purified by fire. This proving of your faith is intended to redound to your praise and glory and honor when Jesus Christ the Messiah, the Anointed One is revealed.
1 Peter 1:7 AMPC

And I will make showers come down in their season; there will be abundant showers of blessing divine favor.
Ezekiel 34:26b AMP

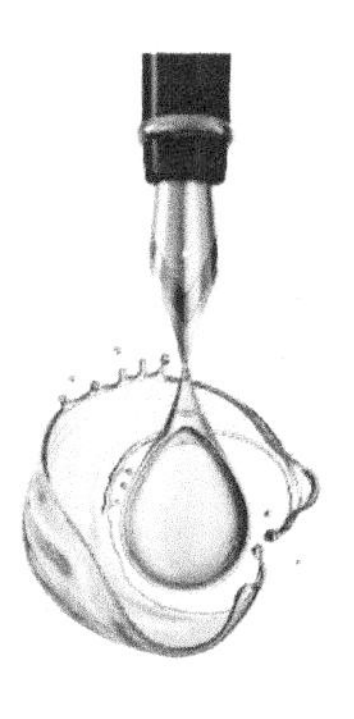

2020

LISTEN FOR THE SOUND

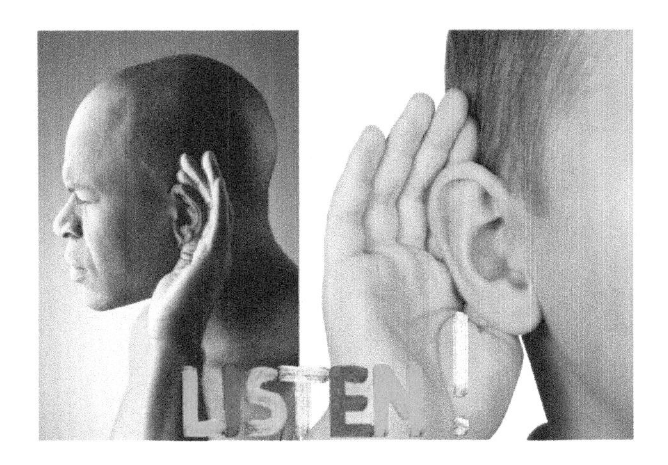

Still yourself and LISTEN. LISTEN for the sound from heaven to be reproduced on the earth. I am the originator of the sound. Become one that I can flow through. Become one that changes the atmosphere with the sound. I release the sound from me to you to be in the earth. Worship Me in the beauty of holiness. Worship Me through the sound. I am coming from within.

It is the sound that breaks many waters. It is the sound of the spirit coming forth. It is greater and it will be known and notable. Atmospheres will change. Everything changes with the sound if you worship Me, you will see the manifestation of My glory. Can I trust you with My sound? Can I trust you to LISTEN?

And I heard a voice from heaven, like the sound of great waters and like the rumbling of mighty thunder; and the voice that I heard [seemed like music and] was like the sound of harpists playing on their harps.
Revelation 14:2 AMP

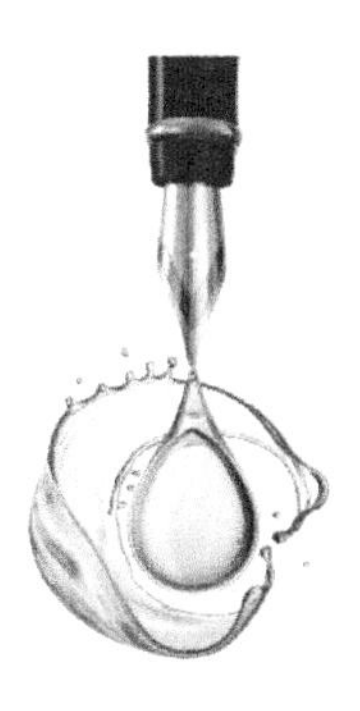

2020

READY WRITERS

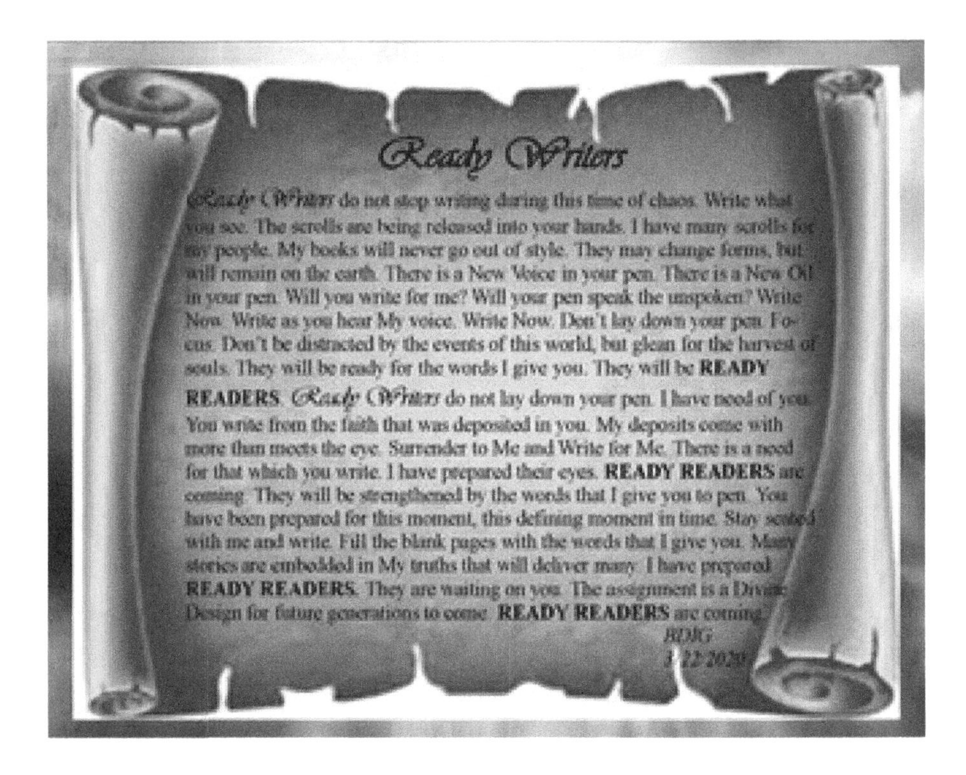

Ready Writers

Ready Writers do not stop writing during this time of chaos. Write what you see. The scrolls are being released into your hands. I have many scrolls for my people. My books will never go out of style. They may change forms, but will remain on the earth. There is a New Voice in your pen. There is a New Oil in your pen. Will you write for me? Will your pen speak the unspoken? Write Now. Write as you hear My voice. Write Now. Don't lay down your pen. Focus. Don't be distracted by the events of this world, but glean for the harvest of souls. They will be ready for the words I give you. They will be **READY READERS**. *Ready Writers* do not lay down your pen. I have need of you. You write from the faith that was deposited in you. My deposits come with more than meets the eye. Surrender to Me and Write for Me. There is a need for that which you write. I have prepared their eyes. **READY READERS** are coming. They will be strengthened by the words that I give you to pen. You have been prepared for this moment, this defining moment in time. Stay seated with me and write. Fill the blank pages with the words that I give you. Many stories are embedded in My truths that will deliver many. I have prepared **READY READERS**. They are waiting on you. The assignment is a Divine Design for future generations to come. **READY READERS** are coming.

BDJG
3-22-2020

Ready Writers do not stop writing during this time of chaos. Write what you see. The scrolls are being released into your hands. I have many scrolls for my people. My books will never go out of style. They may change forms, but will remain on the earth. There is a New Voice in your pen. There is a New Oil in your pen. Will you write for me? Will your pen speak the unspoken? Write Now.

Write as you hear My voice. Write Now. Do not lay down your pen. Focus. Do not be distracted by the events of this world, but glean for the harvest of souls. They will be ready for the words I give you. They will be **READY READERS**.

Ready Writers do not lay down your pen. I have need of you. You write from the faith that was deposited in you. My deposits come with more than meets the eye. Surrender to Me and Write for Me. There is a need for that which you write. I have prepared their eyes. **READY READERS** are coming. They will be strengthened by the words that I give you to pen. You have been prepared for this moment, this defining moment in time. Stay seated with me and write. Fill the blank pages with the words that I give you. Many stories are embedded in My truths that will deliver many. I have prepared **READY READERS.** They are waiting on you. The assignment is a Divine Design for future generations to come. **READY READERS** are coming.

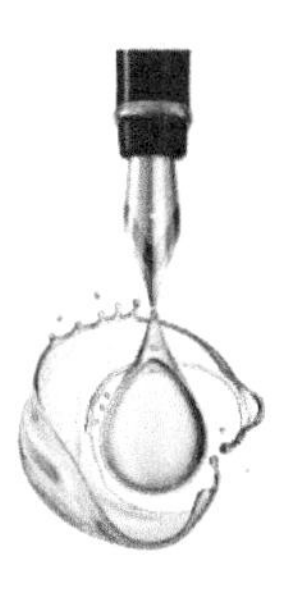

2020

COUNTDOWN

The Countdown has begun, the Countdown to the greater. All of heaven is watching and cheering for this. Look for IT. Look for IT each and every day. Remember that My time is not your time. What is the IT? IT is what I desire and planned for you at this time in your life. Yes, I hold your hand. Yes, I lead you in the path that is prepared just for you. Come closer.

In quietness and stillness will be your strength. Your strength is in My comfort. For I am the Comforter like no other. I am the Comforter of all. Just come to me and rest. Do not ever doubt My presence is with you and that I speak to you. You hear me and know My voice. Trust Me. Rest in Me and you will see the mighty in Me.

"Daniel answered and said, Blessed be the name of God for ever and ever: for wisdom and might are his: And he changeth the times and the seasons: he removeth kings, and setteth up kings: he giveth wisdom unto the wise, and knowledge to them that know understanding: He revealeth the deep and secret things: he knoweth what is in the darkness, and the light dwelleth with him."
Daniel 2:20-22 KJV

"As for us, we have all of these great witnesses who encircle us like clouds. So we must let go of every wound that has pierced us and the sin we so easily fall into. Then we will be able to run life's marathon race with passion and determination, for the path has been already marked out before us."
Hebrews 12:1 TPT

"My sheep respond as they hear My voice; I know them intimately, and they follow Me."
John 10:27 Voice

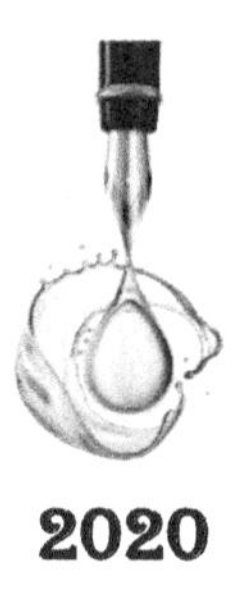

2020

A PATTERN OF THOUGHT

What is your pattern of thought? What is coming in the new time that is before you? Are you thinking the same things as before when I have said that I will do a new thing? You were not designed to think like others who do not believe in Me. It is your believing in Me that makes the difference. So why look and believe what you see and not what you do not see? You do not see me and yet you believe. I am more real than what you do see. Have you not felt my presence? Do you not know when I am in the midst? Have you not heard my voice?

This is the time when I am calling you to think differently as I always have, but know it is for My glory so that all that I have for you will be released. If you who Believe do not think that I can do the impossible, then it will not be done. If you who Believe doubt, then who will Believe? The impossible has always been possible, if you only BELIEVE.

I have been waiting to display My power and glory through you. I ask the question, are you available? If you feel that you lack or are not worthy, just ask, 'Lord, help me, help my unbelief' as my disciples did. You are My disciples that haven been chosen for such a time as this. The fullness of time has come. And I will move among My people like never before.

Look, look up and see the magnificence of this time. Many miracles are waiting for you to only BELIEVE. My thoughts are not your thoughts, and My ways are not your ways. But I will share them with you if you only BELIEVE. The miracles are assigned to you for this season are anxious to be manifested as the evidence of your faith and trust in Me. Only BELIEVE and you shall see the glory of the Lord in the land of the living.

Jesus looked at her and said, "Didn't I tell you that if you will believe in me, you will see God unveil his power?"

John 11:40 TPT

What, what would have become of me had I not believed that I would see the Lord's goodness in the land of the living!
Psalm 27:13 AMPC

Then when the time is right, God will do all that he has planned, and Christ will bring together everything in heaven and on earth.
Ephesians 1:10 CEV

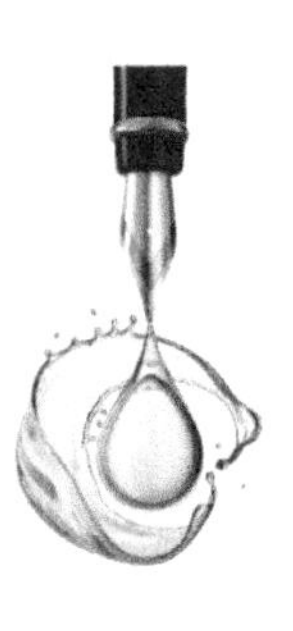

2020

STAND UP

There are some that have been in the School of the Spirit and the Teacher has told them to **STAND UP**. **STAND UP** for the purpose. Some have hesitated, but **STAND UP**. Looking around the class, there are only a few that are standing. They have heard the Voice of the Teacher ad moved on the command. And there were those who mocked. Even though the mockers were in the class, those who stood up were prepared to be separated. Those who mocked will stay in the class for preparation until they receive the revelation to **STAND UP** and heed the Voice of the Teacher.

Who are these that first Stood Up? They have been trained in the waiting. They understood the command to **STAND UP**. It is a timing of the heart. They are purposed to **STAND UP** in this time. Forerunners Stand for the Kingdom before others arrive. **STAND UP** now and go forth for the Kingdom and display the power and glory of GOD in the earth. You do not need a name or a title. The demonstration of the power of God in your life will answer and settle who you are. The order has been given. **STAND UP. STAND UP** and be the beacon of light in the midst of this darkness. The Glory of GOD will shine on and through you. **STAND UP. STAND UP. STAND UP.**

Put on the full armor of God for His precepts are like the splendid armor of a heavily-armed soldier, so that you may be able to successfully stand up against all the schemes and the strategies and the deceits of the devil. Ephesians 6:11

2020

PREPARE TO BE POSITIONED

There is something new coming in the wind and many are being prepared. The old garments of the past are being stripped off. You cannot go into this new season wearing old garments and shoes because of the places that you will walk. This garment has been prepared for you for this time before the foundation of the world. I know you and I know your time. It is Me who has written your book of life and I know every detail of my design.

There are certain things that I did not design you for and the enemy will attempt to trap and lure you into. Seek Me and see My face for the truth and understanding of this plan. It is to keep you stagnant and stale because of the freshness that is coming to you to see and know, to discern the secrets and treasures that I have hidden for such a time as this.

As you come closer, more will be revealed and this is the enemy's plan to keep you from coming closer. Come past the courts, come closer. Come behind the vail. I AM waiting. Let your heart lead the way. It is all prepared. I AM waiting. I AM waiting to prepare you. I AM waiting to dress you in the new garment that will reveal my glory.

There are things prepared to be released. You need to prepare yourself for the arrival, which is imminent. Time has not eroded My plan. For I AM the Lord and I change not. I have not changed my mind concerning what and whom I have designed you be. I AM not surprised by anything about you. For I AM your maker. Now be still, rest in Me, and see My goodness as you continue to walk the path that I have paved just for you. You are not alone. You will be escorted. I AM waiting for you to come up higher and see the vision from a different place. See all that I have prepared for you. Now get ready to position yourself for what is coming. There was never a delay or denial. It was the time and preparation. Are you ready? I AM waiting. Are you ready? Are you ready?

The LORD looked down from heaven upon the children of men, to see if there were any that did understand, and seek God.
Psalm 14:2 KJV

And realize what this really means, we have the privilege of worshiping Yahweh our God. For he is our Creator and we belong to him. We are the people of his pleasure.
Psalm 100:3

There is a season, a time appointed for everything and a time for every delight and event or purpose under heaven. KJV
Ecclesiastes 3:1

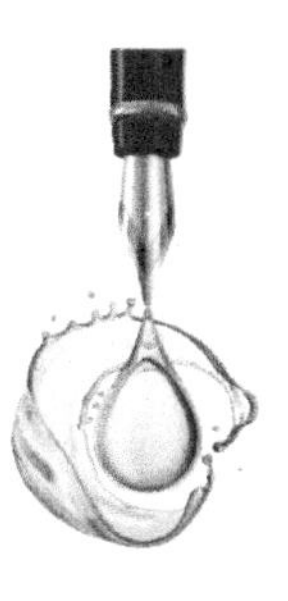

2021

THE LIGHTED PATH

The Lighted Path is one of a step of faith. Every time that you move and step out according to the Word that I have spoken to you, ways are made because you have trusted in My Word. Just taking the step lights the path. Your feet are the activation of faith that is within you. Move towards the open door. Move and Move quickly. Just step. The path is already lit. It cannot and will not be seen until you step. Heaven rejoices when you step because you are showing the faith you have in what you are believing me for.

You have spent enough time in one position. It is time to move. As you move on the lighted path, see the door before you waiting to open. It is your door and no one else can come through. There is much prepared for you. Stay focused and step. Stay on the lighted path. My Word goes before you. Hear My voice and do not delay. We are waiting. Many are waiting. There is a move in your move.

Instead, You direct me on the path that leads to a beautiful life. As I walk with You, the pleasures are never-ending, and I know true joy and contentment.
Psalm 16:11 Voice

Guide me into the paths that please you,
for I take delight in all that you say.

Psalm 119:35 TPT

Consider well and watch carefully the path of your feet,
And all your ways will be steadfast and sure.
Proverbs 4:26 AMP

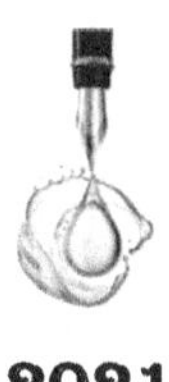

2021

EXPECT ME

I am going to move among you. My people will be distinguished during this time. I am going to move in ways that are and seem to be unusual. It is unusual because I am God. Many have gotten accustomed to the natural and not the supernatural. I Am the Supernatural God and I will do the Supernatural in the earth so that it will be know that I am God and there is no other.

Many have been waiting for this move. Well wait no longer. Wait no longer. It is upon you Now. Even as you read these words released through this vessel, My servant, it is upon you Now. I have ways that you cannot even imagine. For I Am God and there is no other but Me.

Now is the time for you to look and see like never before. Expect like never before. Trust like never before. Your faith is in Expectation. Expect Me to move and I will. Expect to see Me and you will. I will move on your Expectation. Expect. Expect. Expect Me. Expect My visitation. Expect Me to move. Expect. Expect. I Am Expecting you to Expect so that I can move.

I will show My power in your life because you Believe. The wait is over and the time is Now. Expect Me because I Am coming. Do not look for me in the old or ways that you think that I should come. Do not limit Me with your thinking. Elevate your mind and Expect the unusual, the uncommon, and the unprecedented. It is like never before because you have not been this way before. Expect. Expect Me more than ever. You have not been this way before. EXPECT.

Look here, what's done is done and gone. The now is new, and there's hope in the not-yet. I will tell you what's to come, even before the events are brand-new.
Isaiah 42:9 Voice

Jesus looked her in the eye. "Didn't I tell you that if you believed, you would see the glory of God?"
John 11:40 MSG

My soul, wait thou only upon God; for my expectation is from him.
Psalm 62:5 KJV

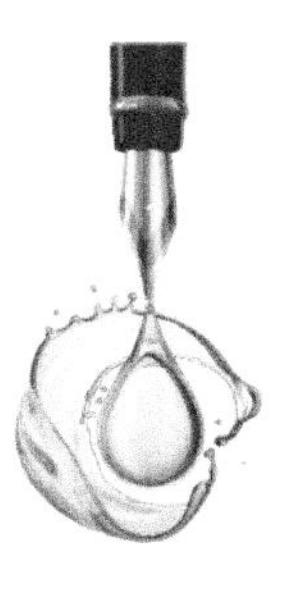

2021

THE GREATER MEASURE

The weight of My Glory is coming to those who are seeking Me. Seeking My face without measure. They continually press Me day and night with their cries from their heart.

Yes, many are seeking but not all are in that place, not all are coming before me with purity. I see the defiled ones and I Am giving them a chance and time of repentance. Repentance must come for the release. Repentance must come. It is crucial to the next phase in the lives of many. Am I not a God that is right there?

And see all that is within and without? I Am not afar off. I Am right there.

The Greater Measure is coming to all who have prepared. Will you be prepared? Are you ready to be prepared? For there is much that I desire to do through My people. I said My people. Those who are longing for my presence. They are the ones longing for the Greater Measure. They have heard about it and now they want to see it and experience Me.

The Greater Measure is not for everyone. It is for those who are diligently seeking. Yeah, many will say that they are seeking, but not. I know the heart of all. I see the heart of all. This is not for boasting. This is a secret that will be displayed to the awe of many because of who I will use to display My glory in the earth. Expect it. Expect it Now.

Live in the Expectation of the Greater Measure. I Am coming for those who are Expecting Me. Are you one? Are you ready? For I Am coming in Greater Measure. Speak it and you will see it. The outpouring has begun, but the Greater Measure is coming. It is coming. You will hear it. You will hear the sound. You will see it. Look up and see. See past the natural and you will see. The Greater Measure is coming.

Shall I move without measure for you? Shall I do that which seems impossible? Shall I? I shall. I shall and you will see and know that I Am the true and living God among you all. Greater is coming. The Greater is coming. Greater is coming. You will experience My presence in the Greater.

Turn to me and receive my gentle correction; Watch and I will pour out my spirit on you; I will share with you my wise words in order to redirect your lives.
Proverbs 1:23 Voice

Am I a God at hand, saith the LORD, and not a God afar off? Can any hide himself in secret places that I shall not see him? saith the LORD. Do not I fill heaven and earth? saith the LORD.
Jeremiah 23:23-24 KJV

And the glory of the LORD shall be revealed, and all flesh shall see it together: for the mouth of the LORD hath spoken it.
Isaiah 40:5 KJV

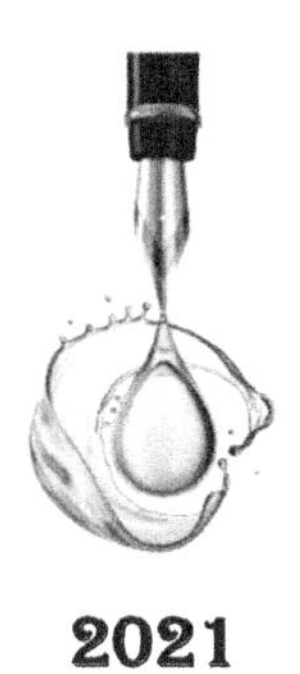

2021

SILENCE
IS A KEY TO LISTENING

When you are silent, you can hear the mind of a person through the words that they speak. You will hear what is in their spirit. They fail to realize that they are creating atmospheres. Language and speech are for creating more than communicating. Communication allows the transfer of thoughts and ideas, which is an element of creativity.

Sometimes it is important and necessary to listen. Develop the art of listening. Become fine-tuned to My voice above all other voices of distraction, even your voice. I see when you listen. I see when you are distracted. I see it all. Now is the time to listen for My instruction. No not miss what I Am saying NOW. When I say nothing, you do nothing. Listen for the rustling in the mulberry trees as David did. I Am speaking loudly now more than ever before. As you wait, as you listen, I Am moving even in the silence. I move on your sound, but I also move in silence.

I know that is hard sometimes to be still and be silent before me. The world has you rushing about, but take time and still yourself in My presence. Enjoy the sweetness of silence. Let Me breathe a freshness, a newness upon you. Feel My breath as I whisper into your ear. In silence, you will hear the whisper, the whisper of My love, the whisper of My heart, the whisper of a secret that I have waited to tell you. It won't take long. Still yourself and know that I Am God. Be still and listen. Be still and listen.

You have prayed and prayed and prayed. Now is the time to listen. Listening is the key to many answers. As you listen, they come forth. There are many keys in listening that I Am releasing that will unlock for the manifestations of what you have asked for. Just wait and listen. Listen for My voice. Listen. I Am always speaking. Learn how I speak, for it is many ways that I choose. Listen. Seek Me and you shall find Me Listen.

The sheep that are My own hear and are listening to My voice; and I know them, and they follow Me.
John 10:27 AMP

Your ears will hear sweet words behind you: "Go this way. There is your path; this is how you should go" whenever you must decide whether to turn to the right or the left.
Isaiah 30:21 Voice

Whoever is of God listens to God. [Those who belong to God hear the words of God.] This is the reason that you do not listen [to those words, to Me]: because you do not belong to God and are not of God or in harmony with Him.
John 8:47 AMP

Therefore, as the Holy Spirit says: Today, if you will hear His voice.
Hebrew 3:7 AMP

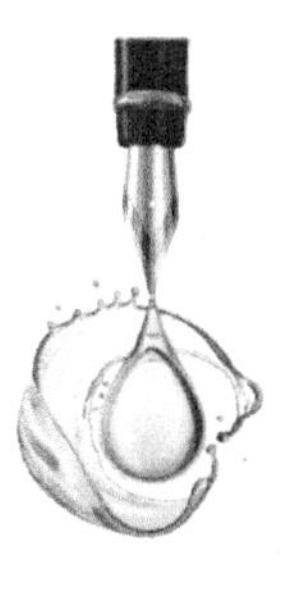

2022

THE MIGHTY ONES

I Am using many instruments of valor in this time. Some are not even aware of how I Am using them. But it will be seen and know by those surrounding them. They will see who is this and how is this. My gift was present with them all the time and they were not aware of their identity.

Today, they will no longer be hidden from view. They are being revealed. Their environment will change as well as the people around them. You did not understand and appreciate the gift that was in the midst of you. I Am rearranging their position to go where they are needed, where there is a need for the display of My power and glory. Where many are believing for the impossible. I Am looking for My Believers, not thinkers of the Gospel. Believe in Me as I have said and you will see My glory in the land of the living. Believe in Me so that the work can be done in My instruments of valor.

This is the time of calling many into the Kingdom. It has always been the time. Every day is the time. I do not want any lost. But I need them to Believe in Me so that they can and will see My love, My power, and My purpose.

I Am calling the mighty ones, the warriors to arise. The ones that are the God Class. God Class warriors move with fearless fury and force against the enemy. They are equipped and they are battleaxes in My land. ARISE FEARLESS ONES. ARISE MIGHTY ONES. I AM that I AM is with you. There are more with you than you can imagine.

Rise Up and go forth to take the land. It is time to possess all that I have given you. Take It, Take It, It is yours. I have prepared a place for my people and it is yours. Rise Up Now and I say Go Forth and possess what is yours, what I have given you. All is waiting for your hand. As you have waited and waited, NOW is the time to move. Sound the alarm. You are battle ready. Take it, Take it by force. ARISE Mighty Ones. ARISE. Come out of the sleep and Arise. You will hear the sound and know that it is time to ARISE!

Thou art my battle axe and weapons of war: for with thee will I break in pieces the nations, and with thee will I destroy kingdoms.
Jeremiah 51:20 KJV

I could tell you how people of faith doused raging fires, escaped the edge of the sword, made the weak strong, and—stoking great valor among the champions of God—sent opposing armies into panicked flight.
Hebrews 11:34 Voice

God standeth in the congregation of the mighty; he judgeth among the gods. How long will ye judge unjustly, and accept the persons of the wicked?
Selah. Psalm 82:1-2 KJV

There will be times, when you're living in the land I've promised to you, that you'll need to fight against people who oppress you. Use the trumpets to sound an alarm. Your God, the Eternal, will remember you, and you will be saved from such enemies.
Numbers 10:9 Voice

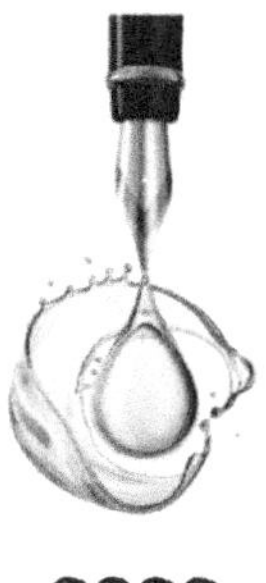

2022

About The Author

Becky DeWitt is an author and coach who works with authors of all genres to help them become bestselling authors. She has written and self-published over 25 titles, in different genres of contemporary fiction, inspirational, and children's books. Becky's writings reveal trial and tribulations from the ordinary everyday perspective as well as edification for the soul.

As the Founder and President of The Blood Drop Inheritance Group, she leads a group that assists emerging authors with formatting and preparing their books for publication. BDIG was created to showcase the anointing of those that God leads her to assist in the publishing process.

Becky combines her vast leadership expertise with her depth of spiritual understanding to reveal life-transforming messages that empower and inspire. She keeps the reader on the edge of their seat and opens the understanding of each reader to drama, suspense, and the godly supernatural.

There is a trilogy that Becky has penned that is a riveting journey through deceit, death, and betrayal which was a way of life. "Contempt, Reasons, and Sabotage" is the journey of the twists and turns of life, taking toil, leaving one in devastation. Only the arrival of a miracle just in time changes everything. Readers experience a maze of mystery and intrigue capturing ones' fascination.

Becky is also an ordained Minister and movie scriptwriter. She has spoken at various writer's conferences and conducted training seminars and has also participated at regional and national book fairs.

Also, she has written feature articles for various websites and print publications and her books are available on Amazon. Some have been translated into French and Spanish. The vision of her company Blood Drop Inheritance Group is to pen those words of inspiration and revelation from the throne room for all generations.

http://www.bdig-beckydewitt.org/
https://www.beckydewittglobal.org/
http://www.authorsden.com/beckydewitt
bloodropinheritance@gmail.com

Popular Trilogy Books

by

Becky DeWitt

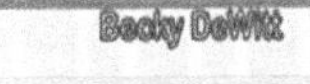

Made in the USA
Coppell, TX
10 September 2022